From A Sinner to A Winner

By Walter J. Miller

From a Sinner to a Winner

Copyright ©2012 Walter J. Miller
Library of Congress: 2012921086

All rights reserved. No part of this book may be reproduced, stored in a retrieval system or transmitted in any form or by any means without the prior written permission of the publishers, except by a reviewer who may quote brief passages in a review to be printed in a newspaper, magazine or journal.

Published by La Maison Publishing, Inc.
Inc.*www.lamaisonpub.com*
ISBN: 978-0-9885902-0-5

Foreword

This is the story of my life! These are poems and letters for the spiritually minded. God inspired these words. They tell how God filled the void in my life doing my trials, tribulations and my addiction. God worked in my life and I thank him.

These poems were written only when I was in the Spirit. This is my time of communication with my God. God filled a void in my life by witting these letters and poems. I thank Him. I love my God for He removed me from a burning fire. I will thank him forever and ever. So, my brothers and sisters let go! It is time to turn to your God for He loves you. Doing my trials and tribulations, He protected me. In the name of Jesus, I thank my God. I want these letters and poems to go out to my brothers and sisters to let them know that God is a forgiving God. He forgave me of all my sins. So, turn to God!

In the name of Jesus, I thank him for giving me these poems and letters to be able to share with others in a written form.

Walter James Miller

Introduction

I was Born Walter James Miller, to Charlie Ben and Thelma Kate Davenport Miller on June 6, 1948. I cannot remember too much of my life in Georgia. We lived in a little town call Leary. Mama left Daddy when I was very small and we came to a small town name Mount Dora. We lived there for a little while. I can remember some of her male friends who would bring us food from a restaurant form across the rail road tracks. Those were some of the best tasting shrimps I had ever eaten. I was the only boy at that time. I was among two girls, Charlie Mae, and Mary Alice. There was talk of a third girl name Johnny Mae. I don't know much about her. I do know I had two sisters for a while.

  I can recall a white man name Mr. Lot. He had Mama's family and some more folks working for him. They worked in those fields from sunup to sundown. Mama would bring some of the vegetables home to feed us with. The folks would make good use of the things that they work in. They would make mattresses, smoke the tobacco and chew it. Mr. Lot tried to show me how to chew tobacco. I would swallow the spit and get drunk.

  Then, we left there and came further south to a little town called Indiantown. Mama started having more children and I came down with a sickness of epilepsy. The old people called them fits but the Bible states that a person born with epilepsy has a demon in them. I think it came from swallowing all of that tobacco spit. Mama had another girl and she named her Brenda Joyce. I did not know that being next to Mom was over. I was not the baby, anymore. I was the only boy in the family, at that time. There was a big responsibility on my shoulder. I had to look after the family, as the man of the house. I got scolded at many times for not being the man of the house. Also, I had to look after those girls. "Awe man", I was just a kid myself. I needed someone to look after me! God did. Mama would take us to the bean and tomato fields to pick those vegetables. I had to work hard because I was the man of the house. My hands were full with the girls. Mama began to send us to church. I liked that because it was a chance to meet other boy and girls my age. I met many friends in that ole wooden church; James Cain, Gene Woodard, Mack and his sisters, Susie and Betty: the Aldridge family. Now, those were pretty girls. I met many friends in that little old town. Mama would let us go to baseball games and to the movies. My job was to look after my sisters wherever they went. I asked myself as I got older, "Who is going to look after me?"

Well, my sickness got worse. Mama would take me to many doctors to cure me of my sickness. I must confess that all things are possible through God. God guided us to the East Coast to a little town called Fort Pierce. I was afraid because I have never seen so many people. Things were the same, however. Looking after the girls and myself was still my job. I knew; however, someone was looking after me and my family other than myself. This power was greater in me than I thought. This power guided and protected me up to this day. He was my best friend, Jesus. Even with my sickness, He was there for me! There were times when I almost ran into cars and almost fell into canals. His loving hands were there. Then, my Friend healed me.

I left my Friend, Jesus for a friend called the World. As time went on things began to change in my life. The girls began to grow-up and so did I. My job came to an end. Mama was still trying to work in the fields to take care of us. Many times she would come home and just go to sleep. The oldest girl, Charlie Mae, would have to cook for the family. Sometimes, it took her forever. I was hungry after playing all day. With just a cookie here and there I wanted some real food. We did not have much but thank God we survived. I grew older still having those spells. Through the love of my

God, I feel that a bad thing turned out good. Whatever happened to my health, it was all God's will. I have many reasons for that statement. I became a man through all my sickness, with the help of Jesus. Mom taught me a lot about the Lord Jesus. I carried His teaching to this day. My mother trusted Him no matter what.

Well, those girls did me a favor. They got married. I knew I was free of them. They would come visit us; however, they had their own family to look after. My sickness was still a part of my life even going through Barber College. I filled my life with many things, such as; sports. I got married. I left the Lord to try and make it on my own. I did fairly well (smile), I thought. I was king of the world. I knew I was king of my destiny. I did not realize that Jesus controlled my destiny. The Lord has been good to me. All of my life through good times and bad He was always there.

Life took a bad turn for me. I got hurt on my construction job. My wife, Althea Clayton Miller, died. Continuing to spiral down, I started using cocaine. This was an addiction that I thought I would never kick. That is when I remembered what Mom said, "Trust in God". It took Him to do it. I prayed day and night for Him to remove that taste from my mouth. God picked me up! There is nothing God cannot do if you trust in Him.

Well, I still hear from my siblings now and then. Mom died and so did Dad. There are many things she taught me that carry me through. She taught me to Trust in God. *Many times when I am writing, I look and think back on all the trials and tribulation I have been through. If it had not been for the love of God where would I be? I still have issues in my life. I need my God to help me. I want Him to help me pull all my sisters and brothers out of the fire. I thank my God for all his love, his mercy and grace. I thank Him for his Son's shed blood that covers me daily. I walk through this life for Him and by Him in the name of Jesus. Lord, please forgive me if I said or done wrong against you. I thank you for being my shelter in the storms in my life. Many times when I was hungry you fed me. O 'Lord you rescued me when I was in trouble. Yes! It takes a good listener to make a good learner. I learned what my mother taught me. Trust in God and do well and He will take care of you.

I WENT FROM A SINNER TO A WINNER BY TRUSTING GOD

W. J. Miller

Table of contents

GOD IS IN CHARGE	19
JESUS BE TRYING TO TELL ME THINGS	20
WORDS OF ENCOURAGEMENT	21
THE SACRED WORD OF GOD	22
TO MY BABY BROTHER	23
TO MY DEAREST CHILD OF GOD	24
LOOKING BACK	25
WITHOUT HIS LOVE	26
FATHER GOD	27
FRUITS OF THE SPIRITS	28
BLOWING IN THE WIND	29
MY LOVE FOR THEE	30
WEIGHING THE ISSUE	31
PRAYER CHANGES THINGS	32
WHAT THE SPIRIT SAYS TO THE CHURCHES	33
SAYINGS	34
THE MILLENNIUM BUG BANDWAGON	35
TO A PEOPLE	36
REDEEMED	37
THE WORD OF GOD	38
TALKING TO MY GOD (Thanking Him)	39
A TRUTH	40
TALKING TO JESUS	41
PREDESTINATED	42
2000 YEARS LATER	43
BEING PATIENT	44

JEALOUSY	44
GIVE ME STRENGTH	45
WHAT HAPPEN TO MY MULE?	45
LET IT BE ME	46
SAYINGS	47
A BELOVED VALENTINE	48
THOSE FIERY DOTS (Visible and Invisible)	49
TALKING TO JESUS	50
IT'S OVER	51
CAN'T STOP	52
ON YOUR DYING BED	53
NOT FAITH	54
I GOT A HOLD ON GLORY	54
UNCLEAN SPIRITS (Demons)	55
GOD'S HAND	56
A CALL UNTO GOD	57
A WORD OF WISDOM	58
BY WHOM	59
TITLES OF ENCOURAGEMENT	59
WHAT A FRIEND	60
PAUL VS PAUL	61
WHO TOOK BARABBAS PLACE?	62
TOUCH ME	63
SPARE NOT	63
BEING THANKFUL (For God's Help)	64
THE RIGHTS FOR THE WRONGS	65
CHANGED	66

SAVING GRACE	67
FALSE SHEPHERDS	68
DON'T ASK! JUST OBEY!	68
I WILL	69
GOD (Of The Four Winds)	70
A LETTER TO MY DARLIN'	70
GOD'S MY PROTECTOR	71
A LOVING MOTHER	72
PASSING BY	73
I TOLD AN ANGEL	74
THE STAGE	75
THROUGH CHRIST	76
CRY NO MORE	77
GOD IS GOOD	78
UNTO YOU	79
SPIRITS	80
I OVERCAME	81
THANKFUL	81
MY STRENGTH	82
THE SEA (Sailing)	83
TRIALS	84
BROKEN PROMISES	85
WHAT THE LORD HAS DONE FOR ME	86
FOR JESUS SAKE	87
GOING THROUGH	88
THAT SMALL! HOW LITTLE!	89
MY EYES HAVE SEEN	90

FILLED TO THE BRIM	91
FRET NOT	91
TEARS OF FEAR	92
VICTORY	93
FLOWERS OF THORNS	94
FIGHT FOR FREEDOM	95
THE LAW OF THE LORD	96
PRAISE	96
THE BIBLE	97
A VOW	97
IN MY CASE	98
MORTAL MAN	99
PRAYER	100
PLEAD MY CAUSE O'LORD	100
O'ISRAEL	101
THAT BRILLIANT FLAME	102
WATCHING AFTER ME	102
NO MORE	103
AN ECHO	104
LOVING THE LORD	104
I AM NOT WORTHY	105
A SOLIDER (My Father)	106
SILENT WORDS	107
G. E. D.	108
THE DEVIL MADE ME DO IT!	109
X-RAY	110
A REVELATION	110

LEGACY OF A LEGEND	111
KNOWING YOUR ADVERSARY	112
FAMILY AND FRIENDS DAY	113
MY HOPE IN THEE	113
UNFOLDING LOVE	114
PRAYER	114
THE SPIRIT	115
POWERS	116
HIS WORD NEVER FAILS	117
DISASTER STRIKE	118
I FELL DOWN	119
THE ROOT OF WISDOM	120
SO MANY THINGS	120
THE FINAL RIDE (Saddle Up)	121
FEELING SECURITY	122
UPON HIS WORD	123
NO SECRETS	124
THE WITHER CROP	124
SAYINGS	126
STAY WITH THE LORD	127
DELIVERANCE	127
FEAR NOT	127
MIND BEATING	128
A SEEDER PRAYER	129
CAST NOT THY STONE	129
CITY LIGHTS AND COUNTRY ROADS	130
THE FOOTSTEPS OF THE POOR	131

I REMEMBER WHEN	132
WAKE UP TO THE SPIRIT	133
MRS. HURSTON	134
THE HOUSE WITH HOLES	135
COURAGEOUS	136
UNTO MY BROTHERS	137
WRONG ARMOR	137
PLANTATION MANNER	138
CRY FOR ME	139
RUNNING FROM GOD TO THE DEVIL	139
I FOUND PEACE	140
THE WEAKER VESSEL	141
THREE BROTHERS	141
THE ANGEL BOX OF PRAYERS	142
CAN'T HIDE HIM	142
DEFENDING JESUS NAME	143
WHAT MY GOD SHOWED ME	144
V.E.T. Venting Eternal Thoughts	145
KEEPING FOCUS	146
RISE UP O'GOD (You are my God)	146
CONFIDENCE	147
THE LORD'S TRAIN	147
FOOTSTEPS IN THE COMMUNITY	148
VIOLENCE	148
CLEAN SHEETS	148
A DIFFERENT	149
BESTOWED	149

A FATHER'S LOVE	150
INSPIRATIONAL THOUGHTS	150
RESURRECTION	151
ENDURE	151
I'M PRAYING FOR YOU	152
SPEAK UNTO MY SPIRIT	152
I GAVE CARE UNTO THE WORLD	153
SECOND CHANCE	153
IN DISPUTE	154
FAMILY TIME	154
LITTLE THINGS	155
ASKING	155
TOOLS	156
SUBMISSIVE (Submitting and Resisting)	156
WORDS	156
TRIBULATIONS	157
LET GOD BE GOD	157
KEEPING MY BROTHER	158
HAVE YOUR WAY	158
TODAY, TOMORROW, YESTERDAY	159
THE UNINSURED DRIVER	160
REVELATION	161
THE MISSING PIECE	162
SPIRITUAL FOOD	163
STEPS	164
FOREVER BURNING	166
12 TIMES 12	167

12 STEPS	168
4 C's - DRUGS OF CHOICE	170
A SINNER'S PRAYER	171
O'STUDENT OF MINE	172
INSTILL	173
I AM A TREE	173
WISE SAYINGS	175
TURN IT AROUND	176
THE CHILDREN	176
PSALMS AND PROVERBS	177
IN THE NAME OF JESUS	178
O'LORD HELP ME	178
FROM BEHIND THE WALL	178
GOD IS OUR REFUGE AND STRENGTH	179
THE FIERY FLAME	179
STRENGTH PRAYER	179
THE VOID	180
THE RUNNER	180
FAITH	181
MAMA'S WORDS (To Mama)	182
TAIL NO MORE	183
CHANGING TIDE	183
WALTER'S GOD	184
STRANGERS NO MORE	185
LUKEWARM	186
I AM YOURS	186
TO DRINK FROM THAT CUP	187

BIBLE PROPHECIES	188
FOR THE BLOOD OF JESUS	189
MALE AND FEMALE FALSE PROPHETS	189
THE DREADFUL ROAD	191
THE SILENT WARFARE	192
WITHIN A NAME	194
TIMES OF FAITH	194
FELLOWSHIP	195
MY ANONYMOUS JOURNEY	196
NO ONE BUT YOU, O'LORD	197
GOD'S WILL	198
BEING CAREFUL	199
THE WHOLE SOUL	200
MY GOD IS	200
LIFE FOR THE LIFELESS	201
THE PRICE FOR YESTERDAY	201
A LETTER TO MY DARLIN'	202
O'JEHOVAH	202
THE WRONG WAY	203
KEEP ON PRAYING	204
THE CREATOR (Second Time Coming)	205
A GOOD MARRIGAGE IS COMMUNICATION	206
BEING A FISHERMAN	207
TELLING IT LIKE IT IS	208
LISTEN TO THE SPIRIT	208
PARALYZED	209
PROMISE KEEPING	210

WHAT A FRIEND	211
TRADITIONALLY SPEAKING	212
FATHER GOD #2	213
PRISON RECORDS	214

GOD IS IN CHARGE

During my triumph years, my God was blessing me in every way! To be and uneducated, black man in my era, I had a beautiful family. I had my own home, a new car, money in the bank and working on a good job. I thought I was on top of the world. Also, I thought this was all good luck. Yes! I then, began to be arrogant. I forgot that it was all God's doing. I hit rock bottom. Not by my God's doing, but by my own selfish desires. I left my God for the world. I did not have the guts to thank Him for the many blessings he had bestowed upon me in my youth and early adult life. Now that I am old, He has put me in a lot that no one can remove but him. I understand that revelation very, very well. Throughout my life, wisdom, knowledge and understanding were given to me. I refused to use His blessings. I chose to use mine and kept falling and falling away from God. One day I prayed to God to lift me up and remove me out of this lot. He showed me who was in control. He showed me who was on top of the world. The world is His footstool. He lifted me up and removed me from that lot. It was a lot of sin and addictions. My God! My God! I truly thank you every day for that blessing. In Jesus name, I thank you for being in charge.

9/3/1999

Walter J. Miller

JESUS BE TRYING TO TELL ME THINGS

Jesus be trying to tell me things but I want listen. Jesus is with me and I know that He is with me. There are things that happened to me that I know only Jesus could have done, but I cannot explain. He is showing me things in the Spirit. My God and I are close. He is my best friend. We walk and talk to each other every day. I thank Him for being there for me; guiding my footsteps and helping me bridle my tongue. Sometimes, I have a hard time with the spirit of truth and controlling my tongue. I pray every day for that change. This demonic spirit within me is keeping me away from my God and cutting off all my blessings. I ask my God to remove this evil spirit. In the name of Jesus, this struggle will help me in my spiritual growth. Why is Satan after me? Why? In spite of all my praying and fasting, he still keeps tempting me on every side. Thanks to God who gave me the LORD, Jesus Christ as my protector. Doing my trials and tribulations, my Jesus protected me. I thank Him. It's hard Lord, trying to serve you. O' Lord, help me to overcome this world and the evil that is within it. Please, O' God, reach out your loving hand and remove this evil from me and I will praise your holy name unto Zion.

9/1999

WORDS OF ENCOURAGEMENT

My brothers and sisters, I did not get here by what I did today. I got here by what I did yesterday. I changed, in the name of Jesus. I pleaded to my God for a change. My brothers
and sisters, whatever you are doing today, if it is not for fullness and the goodness of God, then you need to turn around. Ask for a change and strength. You only have to have a little bit of faith. Ask Him to help you to cultivate that faith. Ask Him to help you make that faith grow so that you can receive His blessing more abundantly. Your God loves you whether you love him or not. Ask Him to help you to run a good race. That is a race of faith. Ask Him for the words of encouragement so that you can get that victory crown. My brothers and sisters these are words of encouragement from a friend to a friend. In the name of Jesus take courage and follow Jesus. He is encouragement to your soul.

9/1999

For the Blood of Jesus

Walter J. Miller

THE SACRED WORD OF GOD

The word of God is sacred. Every word that He spoke is holy. However, there are shunning words and documents that are not true. These revelations are not of God. Even though, He said all scriptures are inspired by him, men try to change and dictate the sacred word of God. Men are leading God's people astray by printing their own words and taking the sacred word of God as their own. Keeping the weak weaker by not strengthen them, but keeping them under their feet as a slave to themselves. They tell them what they are saying comes directly from their god. However, my God said I know you not. Many of God's sheep have been led astray. Many of His shepherds have gone to different pastures, not to the sacred word of God, but away from it. Well, my God said whosoever take a word away from this book would be taken out of the Book of Life. Now, that is the true word of God. They are the sacred word of God.

9/14/1999

Your Child, in the name of Jesus

From a Sinner to a Winner

TO MY BABY BROTHER

How are you doing? Fine I hope. I am sorry that I have not written you before now. Please forgive me. My past is over. The thanks go to my God. Now, I must think of you and my sisters. I love all of you. I am really, sorry that I was not a big brother to you and my sisters. I am truly sorry. I guess that is the way my God had it planned for me. Well, I am doing fine. I hope this letter finds you the same. Now that God is working in my life, I hope that He is doing the same in yours. If not, my brother, look for Him. Find him for He is your best friend.

Well, I do not have much to say. I love you. I hope my God keep you safe until we meet, in the name of Jesus. Trust in your God. My brother, you need to write me so we can build the brother relationship the way brothers are supposing to. Even though I am the biggest, I will listen to you too. I need your advice, too. I hope you are doing the right thing with your life. I hope you know what I am talking about. I am glad you are being your own man and staying out of trouble. Maybe your God is looking out for you. I hope that you thank Him in everything that you do. I praise Him for the good times, as well as, the bad. I cannot say too much right now. Do not be mad at me. May God keep on keeping you safe my brother, in the name of Jesus.

Your Brother

P.S. May God keep blessing you in the name of Jesus and let no weapon form against you prosper.

9/1999

Walter J. Miller

TO MY DEAREST CHILD OF GOD

While laying here thinking of you in the early morning hour, I am praying that you are okay. I think of the times when we have our faults with each other. It is the time we let our adversary run our lives. By letting Him do our thinking, instead of letting his adversary do it for us. If we let his adversary, which is God Almighty, think for us, we would not hurt each other. Because you do not hurt the one you love. You help them. That is the way God shows his love, for you and me. So let us stop hurting each other and start loving one another more. Stop letting our adversary cause us pain. You have the sweetest love I have ever had. Let us keep our faith and trust in God. I know that we are going to make things right with Him so that He will bless us more abundantly. Just keep your head up looking at Him. He is surely looking at you with a smile and clearing our way for us. I love you my dearest child of God.

Love, Walter

10/1/1999

LOOKING BACK

I walk through this life wondering if I am prepared for the next life. I am thinking; did I have the right teachers or did they teach me the proper way to live for that next life. First I will start with mama. Mama taught me what grandma taught her. She tried to teach me the word to their God, His commandments, His truth and love. All this was from her God. Yes Mama taught me respect, virtues and all of their laws. My mind was not on all that stuff back then. All I wanted to do was play marbles and run after the little girls. As I grew and got older things changed. I did not want to uphold the things Mama had taught me. I was led astray by my own foolish desire. I let the world teach me a thing or two. First of all, the world doesn't love you and secondly the world doesn't owe you anything. The world will be the same rather you obey mama or not. After I refuse to listen to Mama, she
turn me over to a man name King Jesus. I began to rebel against Him. Yes, my Brothers and Sisters I was rebellious. No matter how many times I rebel, He accepted me back unto himself. He never stops loving me. I repented and ask for forgiveness. This man took control of my life. There are still a few wounds in my life that I need healed. My God is healing me one day at a time. I think Him. He is my Savior. I thank Mama for turning me over to that man. In the name of Jesus, I don't have to look back.

11/1999

Let No Weapon Form Against Me Prosper

Walter J. Miller

WITHOUT HIS LOVE

With all of God help, I know that I am saved. There's no weapon formed against me that will prosper. In the name of Jesus, I shall overcome. When my adversary is all about me, my God will protect me day and night. I know the blood of Jesus protects and cover me. I thank God for his blood. My brothers and sisters, there's nothing other than the blood of Jesus that can save you. The only way is through the Lord and Savior of the whole world. He is Jesus Christ, God's only begotten Son. So, my brothers, just depend on Him. He is your best friend. Your mother, father, brother or sister can't give you salvation. Only through the grace of God, who gave his only begotten Son, can you receive salvation. He loved the world so much that He let his Son be that ultimate sacrifice. We all should be thankful. We are under the law but God has us under grace. I can't stop thanking Him for his mercy and love. My brothers and sisters, let's return that love by keeping His Word alive and by obeying His Commandments. Let's love one another, carry one another burdens and keep the faith in Jesus.

11/1999

FATHER GOD

Father God, I ask you to help me run this race. I thank you, in the name of Jesus. Father God, I want to win this race. I just don't want to win this race by myself. Father God, I want my brothers and sisters to win in this race with me. If, I run this race and leave them behind, Father God, I would not be going by what you have taught me. I feel that you would send me back after them, to rescue them. That's why I ask you, Father God, to help me run this race. I need to know that you are pleased with me. If I slow down, I can help them along. I want to help save all my brothers and sisters. Father God, keep me in your plan and give me strength. I need all the wisdom, knowledge and understanding you can give me, as I gather in all the lost sheep. I have not forgotten where my strength lies and who have my crown in their hand. Father God, if I stumble, you would be there to pick me up. Father God, you said to love my brothers and sisters as you love me. I would not love them, if I leave them behind. Those are your Words, Father God. All my life I have been trying to do your Word and live by them in Jesus name. O' Father God!

11/1999

Walter J. Miller

FRUITS OF THE SPIRITS

Speaking of spirits and of its fruits, it can get very, very deep. But speaking of the Fruit of the Spirit, it is no secret they are common everyday things. There are laws against other spirits and its fruits. There are no laws against the Fruit of the Spirit. They are Love; there are no law against love for God is love. Joy; it's a wonderful thing to have joy for the love of Jesus is joy. Peace; my God said keep it at all cost among your fellowman. Longsuffering; we must endure longsuffering for Jesus suffered for our sins. Kindness; God was kind to every one sinner or not. That's part of His spirit. Goodness; for the goodness of his love, He gave his only begotten Son so that we can have life more abundantly. Faithfulness; it's a bond when you hold someone to a belief or having faith in them. He said that he would send a comforter and we kept the faith in his faithfulness. Gentleness; God was gentle with us because he could have destroyed the whole world. Instead, He was in full control for he had Self-control over the Fruit of the Spirit.

11/99

BLOWING IN THE WIND

Is not your love for your God blowing in the wind? My brothers and sisters, the answers you are seeking from your teachers, are they not blowing in the wind? Just like your faith in your god. Get a real God that can't be blown about. He is everywhere. If, you look under that or over yonder, He is there. My Savior is not blowing in the wind. Just trust in Him and your faith will not be blowing in the wind. How many roads must a sinner go down before they are called a child of God? The answers are not blowing in the wind for Jesus has the answer. My sisters and brothers don't let your life away from Christ keep blowing in the wind. All you have to do is go to Him. He is right there waiting on you. I can recall how my life was blowing in the wind. I was living in sin, my life was not solid in the Lord and my life was really blowing in the wind. Ask God for a solid foundation in your life. From a friend to a friend, let God blow in your life not in the wind.

12/7/99

Put your trust in the Lord and he will drive out all the wickedness in your life. He will put a smile on you that no man can remove. For the Lord is your Shepherd you shall not want.

Walter J. Miller

MY LOVE FOR THEE

Let the world scorn me. Let them even persecute me. No matter what they do to me, it will not take away my love for thee. For I love thee beyond all means. You are my strength and my protection during the storms. O' Jehovah you give me my daily bread. You have forgiving me my debts as I forgave my debtors. O 'Lord, Jehovah you help me not to be lead into temptation and you delivered me from evil. O' Jehovah you gave me your whole armor to girt my loins with the truth of your only begotten Son. My Lord and Savior, Jesus Christ. O' Jehovah Nissi you are my banner. You prepared me for readiness by putting on me the shield of faith. Because of my love for thee, I have put on the helmet of salvation. You gave me your sword which is the Word of God. O 'Lord you said that you would protect me through my prayers. I keep on praying unto you O' Jehovah Shammah for you are always there for me. Your love for me is so great. It's a declaration of thy kingdom. Your power is ever lasting. I will give you the glory and the praise. That's my love for thee.

12/07/1999

I waited patiently for the Lord, then, He answered my prayers. He heard my plea for help. He pulled me out of my addiction for I put all my trust in the Lord. He taught me a new song to sing so that those who see this will take warning they, too, can know how I love thee and
Him me.

WEIGHING THE ISSUE

My Brothers and Sisters,
Are there mornings when you wake up feeling different than when you went to bed? You feel tired or envious, even radical, however, you humble yourself. Could that spirit have went in the wrong direction and did not make it back in time? Could your spirit get mixed up in the administering spirits by different angels or gods? If you wake up with a different spirit, what went wrong? Did you not pray unto God for protection? Did you not ask Him to protect you through the night? So that demon won't take your spirit. There are a lot of unfamiliar spirits out there just waiting on a soul to devour. My brothers and sisters don't think your guardian angel was laying down on the job. God don't hire lazy angels or make sorry ones, either. Did you pray for the right protection or did your adversary step in on your prays? Was there a misunderstanding on your behalf of how to pray? An unstable thinker and a double minded person can be a real threat to your sanity and to your prayers, when going before God.

12/9/99

Walter J. Miller

PRAYER CHANGES THINGS

You are out there living in sin. You do not know which way to turn. All you have to do is pray for prayer changes things. When you are down and out, you need to pray unto Jehovah. That's where all your help comes from. Prayer changes things. Yes! My brothers and sisters, pray unto God. He is the only one that can change things. So, be of one sober mind. God hears your every cry. Just keep on praying, for prayer changes things. In the name of Jehovah, let no weapon form against you. Learn the ability of your Savior, Jesus Christ. He died for us all, so our prayers can be answered. You can do all things through the power of God who strengthen you. You are an overcomer of the world. We all should thank God for giving His only Son, so that we can have life more abundantly. He listens to our prayers. Prayer really changes things. Jesus had to pray unto the Father. What about us? Let us not forget to pray. Keep on praying, for prayer changes things.

12/29/99

Do not criticize or judge one another for God, Jehovah is the only judge. Keep the faith, hold on and be patient, until Jesus return. He will return soon and very soon.

WHAT THE SPIRIT SAYS TO THE CHURCHES

This is what the spirit says! He who listens to what the spirit of Jesus is saying to the churches should hear the Word of God. Those without an ear can't hear the true Word of God. I am not just talking about the physical ear. I am referring to those who are not born again, those who are not a new creation unto God and those who are not anointed with the Holy Spirit. Some born again Christians are not willing to listen to what the Spirit is saying to the churches. They, like the children of Israel, are rebellious. They are against what the Holy Spirit is saying to the churches. They feel as if they are masters of their own lives. This is a dangerous position to live. There are Christians who are willing to listen to what the Spirit is saying to the churches. The scriptures say we should be doers of the Word, not hearer only. Faith without works is no good. Those who overcome by listening to what the Spirit is saying to the churches will have the right to eat from the tree of life and be with God. They would have a place in God's kingdom in paradise forever and ever. Hear what the Spirit has to say to the churches.

12/9/99

Walter J. Miller

SAYINGS

There are no heroes, just watchman for the Lord. Be not asleep when He returns. I believe any man, who don't have or accept the Lord Jesus Christ as their Savior, is already dead. Through his love, man live. He is eminent to the world. His word and power is great.

Satan is no hypocrite. He is true to his game and his aim. That aim is to search and destroy. He is aiming straight at you, my brothers and sisters. Be no hypocrite. Be true to your game of serving the Lord. If not, woe unto you.

He is the storm before the storm. He is the middle of the wheel. He is the shield before the shield. He is love where there is no love. He is light before the darkness and light after the darkness. My brothers and sisters, yes, God is the power and strength in everything. He is all in all. He is over the highest and the lowest. He is the first and the last. He is the power and strength, in the name of Jesus.

12/30/99

THE MILLENNIUM BUG BANDWAGON

Everybody is jumping on the bandwagon of this 2000 millennium ordeal. The book of Ecclesiastes says there's nothing new under the sun. This same millennium has been before. Just open your eyes. Study and show yourself approved. Don't let anyone betray you. People are trying to deceive God's Saints with the millennium bug. Y2K is something that man has made. The Y2K bug is really bugging the Saints of God. Saints, are you not listening to what the Spirit is saying to the churches? No man and I mean no man knows not the hour or day the Lord is to return. People are getting rich on the people of God. So, let's not be misled by man decisions. When God is to return, no man knows. Man doesn't control God, God control man. Some of my brothers and sisters are being betrayed by this millennium bug. They are jumping on the bandwagon too. They have documents that will tell you the same thing I am saying. If only you would read it. That document is the Holy Bible, which is the true Word of God. It holds the true revelation of the Almighty God. READ IT! Leave God's returning to God and not to man. Whenever God returns, will you be ready? You must repent, repent, repent of all your sins and accept God as your Lord and Savior. When He comes, rather it is today or tomorrow, will you be ready? Repent and He will receive you unto himself whenever He returns. So, don't let yourself be deceived by the devil. He is a bug!! Spray him down with the Word of God

12/30/99

Walter J. Miller

TO A PEOPLE

This is a letter to a people. Those people are the Saints of God and Sister Eloisie. As I sit here as a new born babe unto Christ, the millennium is just four days into its stay. We both have a long way to go. For me, I know that I will have both good and bad days alike. Through the grace of God, I will prevail, for from Him comes all my strength. In the name of Jesus, where all my help comes from…Through Him, I can do all things. I have the ability of Him that is in me. He will let no weapon form against me. In the name of Jesus, I am changed. My God had pity on me, took my hand and changed my life. I thank Him every day. He gets the glory and all the praise. I just want all the Saints of God to know that even they are already in God's plan. We still have a long way to go. So, Saints of the most high God, be patient. God is not finish with you yet. So, pray at all times without stopping. That is what your adversary wants you to do. Worship and praise God only, in the name of Jesus. He is your defender and protector. People wake up and look around you. See the Spirit of the Almighty moving among you. If you have an ear then listen to what the Spirit is saying to the churches. Let's turn Satan's weapon upon himself. Saints, it's time for all of us to come together and fight this warfare.

01/04/2000

From a Friend to a Friend to a People

REDEEMED

Because of the blood of Jesus, I am redeemed from my affliction. I ask God to let all my organs, tissues and muscles function in perfection of the way He created them to work. I pray that God's word be establish in me, for I know that His Word, for I have been redeemed. All my past is behind me. My God has forgiving me and all my dark days are over. Jesus came into my life. He is light. My concern now is that I have been redeemed, in the name of Jesus. I thank Him. O' how I love Jesus and praise the Lord, for He is my best friend. I went out into the desert where my God redeemed me. Out there in the wilderness, I cried out unto my Lord for mercy. He had pity upon me and rescued me. I was living in sin and my addiction was ever before me. He forgave me all of my wrongs. He redeemed me. Now that I am at peace with myself, I am happy all day long. I am redeemed!

01/06/2000

The blood of Jesus covers me at all times!

Walter J. Miller

THE WORD OF GOD

As I wrote down the words God has giving unto me, I receive them with joy. He said to share these words with my brothers and sisters. These words are the words of truth because they were from the Almighty. First, I must acknowledge and obey these words, myself. Then, my brothers and sisters will accept me along with God's words. They will understand why I am giving them these words. They must obey the Word for themselves, in order to receive the blessings God has for them. God will bless everyone that listens unto His word. I did! God's word is something no one should ever forget. God's word is like a necklace of gold around your neck. So, Saints and Children of the most high God, study to show yourself approved unto God. Keep His word in your heart and show it among your fellowman. Let it shine daily as you walk through this world. God's word has made you an overcomer of this world. He has not let any weapon form against you. God's word has strengthened you so you can do all things through Him. God's word has giving you the ability to do, in the name of Jesus. My brothers and sisters, fret not thyself of evil doers, listen unto and do the word of God.

01/08/2000

Study to show thyself approved unto God, a workman that needs not to be ashamed, rightly dividing the word of truth. II Timothy 2:15

TALKING TO MY GOD (Thanking Him)

Dear God,

As I look back on my past and all my trials and tribulation, I am blessed. I am blessed for having a God like you. I can talk to God face to face. A God that is so loving and so forgiving. God I thank you. God I thank you for waking me up this morning. God I thank you for my eye sight, my health and strength. I thank you for the roof over my head and the stove that I cook on. O'God, how I love thee for the clothes you have put on my back. O'God, I thank you for everything, in the name of Jesus. O'God, I thank you for giving your life for me and being that ultimate sacrifice. You are the precious lamb. O'God, keep me under your wing. In the name of Jesus, I thank you. O'God, touch my brothers and sisters. Heal them of their affliction and addiction. O'God, teach them your ways and statues. Listen, O'God, to their plea for they are crying out unto you. Hear them. O'God, open their eyes so they can see your glory. O'God, help them by reaching out your everlasting hand. O'God, fill the pits that are in with your everlasting hand. I will praise you upon your holy mountain and worship you all day long. I thank you for listening to your servant.

01/11/2000

Walter J. Miller

A TRUTH

Hurting tears are tears that become drying tears. They were tears of joy as the lies become truth because He is alive. They said He died, yet, He is alive. He took a three day rest and on the third day He rose and went back to work. He got a raise. Yes! He got a raise from his Father. He received a raise of all time. HE received a raise above all. He was the biggest executive in the world. Unknowingly, the world wanted Him dead. The world tried but He was untouchable. He was loyal to his Boss, his Firm and his Employees. He gave word to the people that He would bless them richly. He did it all for us so that we can be heirs of His will and wealth. A wealth his Father gave Him. He wants us to have a share of his wealth. All we have to do is keep working for His cause. That cause is to love one another as He loved us. His Father loved us first by giving us his only begotten Son. In the name of Jesus, we are rich, rich in faith. We have a richly faith that will give us eternal riches and a room in his Father's house. If it were not so, He would not have said so. That's a truth.

01/12/2000

I let myself be unhappy over a mortal, by disobeying my God. He has a happiness that no mortal can give.

TALKING TO JESUS

Dear Lord,

It's been a year since I met you (January 13, 1999). I thank you, in the name of Jesus. You pull me out of that burning fire. You changed my life and I am redeemed. With the blood of Jesus, I know that I am saved. O'God, I love you. Keep me Lord, Jesus. Your name only can save me. Amen! You are my umbrella, my protector, my rock and my salvation. My soul waits for the day of your return. God is coming to rescue me from the world. I was going through my trials and tribulation. Sin had me against a wall and for his love He came and rescued me. My friends dug pits for me to fall in but He came and showed me around those pits. O'Lord, I love you with an agape love. A love I can't explain. I keep hearing Psalms 62; all the days of life I will depend on God alone because He redeemed me. I know that God has changed me, in the name of Jesus. Yes, my brothers and sisters, talk to God face to face as you would a friend. He is always waiting on a friendly voice. Good or bad, trust in God. Keep Psalm 62 in your heart as long as you live.

01/15/2000

Let the good fruit be brought forth, in the name of Jesus.

Walter J. Miller

PREDESTINATED

Wait for the Lord, my brothers and sisters, don't try to bring Him back before time. Just be prepared for His return. Man is a predestinated creature; his life is ordered by God. Human has always been a predictive creature. That's why God gave him a mind to do as he pleases. God gave man choices to serve him or not to serve him. Man's whole life is already predestine. God's Spirit is already upon you because you were made in his image. He is Spirit and his Spirit dwell within you. You can, however, let your adversary take control. Your adversary will control your destiny straight to hell. Let God lead your life, my brothers and sisters. He has it all sum up. God has it all worked out. If, you will read His word (the Bible) and do His will and not yours. Jesus loves you. You have to obey Him. The life He has predestined for you is full of blessings. Let those who predict, predict! Let those who prepare, prepare! God has man's destiny in his hand for man is predestinated.

01/15/2000

2000 YEARS LATER

Many years has come and gone. Two-thousands years later, man is still a vicious creature and very unproductive unto himself. Man was created by a higher power which is the almighty Jehovah. He made man to be like Himself to share his image. The Almighty gave man his spirit. He gave him as free will. Man became predictive and learns how to be unproductive. He began to unequal himself from his fellowman. He became proud. Two-thousand years later he began to enslave his brothers and sisters with his religious ideas and way of thinking. Their attitude changed toward their maker. Two-thousand years later man still hold onto that same attitude that he is better than his brother. God created all men equal; some taller, some shorter, some bigger or some smaller. They all have the same mind, spirit and same measure of faith. Two-thousand years later those who subject themselves to that attitude have the mind of Lucifer, when he said, "I will be like the Almighty. I will ascend unto the heavens and sit upon God's throne." This attitude 2000 years later still rings out. God brought Satan down to the earth and today he is still trying to destroy God's people. Two-thousand years later, God is still in charge. The cry of the millennium man is still trying to be better than his brother. Man has his religious ideas, thoughts and predictions that he is better. How can the pot be better than his maker? How can anyone be better than the next 2000 years later?

01/16/2000

Walter J. Miller

BEING PATIENT

O'Father, give me the patient to try and understand your creation. They were made by you and so was I. you have been very, very patient with me through the years. When I was going through my trials and tribulation, I thank you for being patient with me. Dear God, please teach me to be patient with my brothers and sisters, in the name of Jesus. Help me to bare their burden in your name. I pray, O'Lord, that you teach them to be patient with me. AMEN.

01/16/2000

JEALOUSY

Jealousy is the down fall of man. Man is a predictive creature. He will predict that he can do this and do that, no knowing that the Almighty holds all his cards. That is where all his strength comes from. By him not loving his brother, that's were his jealousy sit in. His hatred for his fellowman gets the best of him because he knows not of God. God is love. Be thy not jealous, my brothers and sisters.

01/16/2000

GIVE ME STRENGTH

O'Lord, give me strength. I need strength to lead my family in the right direction. My family is your children. O'Lord, help me to be a good husband and a wonderful father. In the name of Jesus, give me strength! O'Lord, most of all give me understanding to show them what love really is. Give me wisdom, O'Lord, to guide my family toward you. Give me knowledge to help my family in times of trouble. Give me strength to keep my family together. O'Lord, help me to make the right decision in everything concerning my family. O'Lord, help me to keep them spiritually minded, at all times, in the name of Jesus. O'Lord, bless my family that we may grow up together in your house and in our house. Give us all of your love. We will praise your holy name in our house and in yours. Give me the strength that you gave Moses, Sampson, and Joshua. O'Lord, be the middle of my wheel. Be my household. O'Lord, help my family to serve you. Give me strength!

01/17/2000

WHAT HAPPEN TO MY MULE?

I have some questions. What happen to my mule? What happen to your promise? What happened? I need my mule to plow my land. I need my mule to ride out of this valley. What happen to my mule? I can't ride no horse because he goes to fast and make my butt sore. What happen to my mule? I need my mule, because she rides real smooth. What happen to my mule?

01/22/2000

Walter J. Miller

LET IT BE ME

Dear Lord,

I praise your name and worship the day that I found you. O'Lord, I remember in the Bible that you ask, "Who will go out into the world of the lost". I said, "Let it be me." O'Lord, you ask, "Who will drink from this bitter cup and who will bare this cross that I carry?" Let it be me. Lord, you said not to worship no other God but to worship you only. O'Lord, you said if I ever needed a friend, you said to let it be you. Lord, you are the best friend that I ever had. When your only begotten Son said, "If it's your will O'Father, I will be that ultimate sacrifice." He said, "Let it be me." O'Lord, you also said, "Who will feed my sheep? Who will heal the sick?" I said, "Let it be me." Lord, I want to be your cup bearer and messenger, in the name of Jesus. Let it be me.

01/22/2000

SAYINGS

O' Leopard, O' Leopard rid thyself of thy spots. Go down to the river and clean thyself. Wash thyself in the river and be clean of thy spots. O'Leopard, O'Leopard, you can't hide from thy maker. I can still hear John crying, saying, "Repent, repent and be baptized, in the name of Jesus." Prepare your way for the Lord. Let's come off that old dreadful road of sin and repent for His kingdom is near.

The cured demon did get saved by the word of God. Did you hear me? He was healed of his affliction, his horror and his sins. He went back and told his brothers and sisters. They were amazed. Jesus cured a demon posse man. He screamed as he was being healed. You can be healed, also.

Say the word, O'Lord. Speak unto my body, O'Jehovah, so that I may be healed. Just say the word, O'God that my sins may be forgiving and I will praise thy name. Heal me, O'Jehovah, please say the word.

You are better than the sparrow. Look not, my brother and sisters, at your affliction and thy hunger. Look at the sparrow. Are thy not better than the sparrow? The Almighty takes care of the needs of the birds of the air. Are thy no better than the sparrow?

02/04/2000

Walter J. Miller

A BELOVED VALENTINE

To me, a beloved Valentine is someone who you would not mind asking, "Will you be mine." Someone you would not mind spending a lifetime. Blessed are the few and many. There is not one as sweet as mine. I think how much you mean to me. I know that I am blessed. Day and night, my beloved Valentine, you are on my mind. Beloved Valentine, before you break my heart, may I ask, "Will you be mine, so that I can have a Beloved Valentine."

02/10/2000

THOSE FIERY DOTS (Visible and Invisible)

If you don't have on the whole armor of God, those fiery dots will get you down. Those fiery dots can be visible and invisible. They all can be dangerous to your soul. They have powers that you can't control; powers of darkness and powers that are not of this world. Brothers and Sisters, be not betrayed by people of this world. Don't mess around with those fiery dots. You can't control them. That's why I say put on the whole armor of God for He will protect you. *For God so love the world that He gave his only begotten Son* for this cause. God gave you choices to put on that armor or not. I give you fair warning not to get involve. Jesus died for you. Stay away from demonic followers for they will carry you straight to hell. Put on and keep on the whole armor of God. He will protect you. He will be your shield when those fiery dots are shot at you. That shield of faith will keep you, at all times. Many unseen things can be seen with the blood of Jesus. So, keep the faith in all you do. From a friend to a friend, in the name of Jesus, pray. Those fiery dots are all over, just look around. They are visible and invisible. Jesus has set you free with his blood, by dying on the cross.

02/16/2000

Walter J. Miller

TALKING TO JESUS

O' Heavenly Father, I praise your name. I thank you for healing me for once I was lame. You are the Father of my mother, father, sisters, brothers and all my friends. I surely thank you for being everything to me. You are my shelter and my shield. You gave your only begotten Son for me. I want to serve you, O' Lord, until the day you call me home. If it was not for Jesus, where would I be? Father God, I love you. You loved me first by giving your only child for your servant. I have life more abundantly. Father, teach me how to love my brother and to walk in your ways. The first time in many years, I am at peace within myself. I feel so blessed by the love of God. I feel good for the love of God has me feeling this way. I wish I can express how I feel right now. If you know what I know, you would go and get some of Jesus. I go through my hard times but my Jesus is always there. When I am lonely, He comforts me. He taught me how to be content. Yes, Jesus loves me for the Bible tells me so. That's why I love talking with Jesus. He is my best friend. He is some one that I can tell all my troubles to. Again, I say, I love talking to Jesus.

02/17/2000

IT'S OVER

Well, well it's over! I hope that I have Elousie to myself for once. We have buried her first husband, Jimmy. There is a second in line; however, I feel a little better waiting on number two. Then she will be all mines, a dream come true. I caught pure hell for that man being dead. I could not get any sense out of Elousie. I had to be very, very patient. She was going through something. I got jealous but I knew that she loves me. So, I let her have her way. Now that it's over, I am glad for the both of us. Thank you Jesus, I hope that I don't be there for my day. I don't want to get jealous at myself or see her cry over me the way she did Jimmy. She cried real tears. She made me feel good after it was all over. Knowing it's over now; both of us can get some sleep, in the name of Jesus. The sermon for that day was, *Are you ready when the Lord comes for he can come as a thief in the night?* Are you ready my brothers and sisters? Is your house in order? If not, you better do some house cleaning! What I mean by that is to repent, repent! Elousie, Walter, Elijah and Almando are you ready? Tell all of your friends to repent for the time is near. My God is coming back. Have you repented of your sins and ask God to forgive you? Pray unto the Almighty Jehovah that He let you walk with Jesus. According to the word of God, you can lay down your burden to the Lord. So, Elousie, Walter, Elijah and Almando, let's repent unto God.

02/26/2000

Walter J. Miller

CAN'T STOP

To my Brothers and Sisters:

The Lord is good. His mercy is great and his love is forever. That's why I don't want to stop praising Him. I can't stop worshipping the Lord. Every day I praise his name because He died for me. I have been changed through the blood of Jesus. I am covered in the blood, thanks to Jesus. Let no other blood cover you or surround your life but the blood of Jesus. I don't know about you, my brothers and sisters, I can't stop serving the Lord. Sometimes in life my people things happens. You have to think twice sometimes before you speak. The devil will take control of your tongue to keep you from saying God's Words. That's why, I say be careful with your tongue and let not your anger cause you to sin. I am going to wait on the Lord. Being patient is the best way. God knows how much you can take. He will put no more on you than you can bear.

02/28/2000

ON YOUR DYING BED

There's an old saying that goes like this, "On my dying bed". Remember that saying? Sometimes you would swear to that saying. This saying meant that you were serious. You meant what you were saying. Mama told me that it means something different. She said the things that you do to people and don't ask for forgiveness or to forgive them, then you will see all this on your dying bed. She said, if you never called upon the name of the Lord, there is no better place to call Jesus than your dying bed. What a time to call the name of the Lord. It's better to call upon the name of the Lord before that dying day. My brothers and sisters, call upon the name of the Lord while you live. On your dying bed He will be there beside you. Death comes like a thief in the night. Death is everywhere; right around the corner, in some cases across the road. It has no special places to come. Some people get blessed on their dying bed. Some never met the Lord until their dying bed. Find the Lord before that dying day. If not, He will meet you on your dying bed.

03/01/2000

Draw near unto God

Walter J. Miller

NOT FAITH

Father, as I move on in this life, lift not thyself away from me. Help me to stay close to you. Not faith alone will keep me under your wing. I know that I will prevail as I hold onto your hand. Not faith alone will keep me in your court where I belong. Not faith got me where I am today. It was all the love of God. Faith without works is dead. Keep yourself hid in the Lord for He will protect you. Not faith but his love is what makes you want to keep the faith in Him and do well.

03/02/2000

Keep the faith and do well.

I GOT A HOLD ON GLORY

I have a hold on the Lord, which is my glory, as long as I keep my faith in God. I am going to glorify the Lord for He is worthy of all my praise. I will worship Him until He returns again. The Lord redeemed me. By His blood I know that I have been redeemed. I thank God for rescuing me from the world. If, the Lord said I have been changed, it's all good. If the Lord said it, you can count on it. I thank God for healing me. I praise His mighty name. The Almighty Jesus Christ is my Lord and Savior. Keep a hold on the Lord and never let go, No matter how hard your trials and tribulations are hold on to God. God's mercy is forever, Give Him the glory for He knows how much you can bear. Keep on praising the Lord and worship Him daily. He will bring you through. Hold on my brothers and sisters. I got a hold on glory.

03/07/2000

UNCLEAN SPIRITS (Demons)

Demons are very real according to the scripture. The word is not found in the Bible. The word means evil spirit or devil (a.k.a. Satan or Lucifer). They have bodies like men for they are wise and intelligent. They have miraculous powers. Do not possess anything of them for it is forbidden. In the name of Jesus, stay away from them. Cast them out. They can deceive you. They will betray you through man. Through the doctrinal error of man, unclean spirits have creep into man's life. Man became believers of these seducing spirits. Man was unfamiliar with these spirits. They toyed with them in the wrong way. That's why it's best to keep on the whole armor of God to fight against these demons. The influences they have on mankind are great. They call themselves of Christ but they are not. Study, my brothers and sisters, about these unclean spirits for they are demonic. They are in this world and waging warfare against God's Saints. The bible says entertain strangers for you might be entertaining an angel. It did not say good or bad. They are germs, sickness and diseases. My brothers and sisters, ask your God to teach you about these demons. They are works of the Chief Demon, Satan. He is, also, known as Lucifer. They are angels that have fallen from God and want you to be like them, away from God. Jesus is coming back to bound and rebound those unclean spirits.

03/07/2000

Walter J. Miller

GOD'S HAND

God's hand has lead and guided many prophets and people in the right direction. During this time, they did not know which way to go. He led people such as, Noah, Abraham, Isaac and Jacob. Now, O'Lord, I am asking you to lead and guide Walter in the right direction. God lay your hand upon Walter and show him the right way to go. God's hand has always been mighty among his people. Give me the strength to climb in the name of Jesus. Please Jesus, ask your Father to lay his hand on me. I pray day and night for God's hand to help me in my trials and tribulations and to help me stop my sinful ways. My spirit is vex, O'Lord, heal me of my afflictions. God you took away my addiction, take away this affliction. Lay your hands upon me. Nobody but you Lord can do this with your mighty hand. Put your spirit in me and bless me. O'God teach me how to love others and show me how to fellowship with my brothers and sisters. Please Father, I need your hand in my life. God's hand is the only hand that can make you fall or stand. It's God's Hand!

03/13/2000

From a Sinner to a Winner

A CALL UNTO GOD

O'Father,

I lay and wept all night, however, I know you will bring me joy in the morning. Blessed be the name of the Lord from which my help comes from. I thank you Jesus. Once I was lost but the Almighty found me and redeemed me. I gave my God a call and He answered my call. He looked upon my affliction and my addiction. The Almighty Jehovah forgave me all of my past sins and put a new song on my lips. I thank God for listening to my cry. I will worship Him and praise his name forever. My brothers and sisters, if you are in need and have no one to turn to, turn to God. Give a call unto God for He will be there for you. I gave a call unto God and He look at my sickness and healed me. I have faith in my God. All you have to do is ask and He will give it unto you. My affliction was too great for me to handle. I carried my pain and my hurt to God. He gave me a new start, in the name of Jesus. I am at peace with myself. If you need peace in your life, give a call unto God.

03/16/2000

Greater is he that call upon the name of the Lord.

Walter J. Miller

A WORD OF WISDOM

Think not of thy own ways but think of the ways of Jesus. Let not your ways lead you to hell but let your ways lead you toward God. Don't think of your own selfish desire but the desire of God. His ways are good. He will make all of your ways good, if only you depend on Him. Trust not on your own understanding but the understanding of God. To know all this you must get wisdom, knowledge and understanding. Most of all you have to study the word of God. The Bible is the true document of word. Study it and show yourself approved. In the beginning He was the Word and He will be that same Word in the end. God will never change, my brothers and sisters. Love God with all your heart and all your soul. Praise Him daily and worship Him the rest of your life. Jesus is the good Shepherd and we are His sheep. He will watch over us as long as we stay in His care and in His pasture. In other words, let Jesus build a fence around you and your life. From a Friend to a Friend, I have giving you a word of wisdom.

03/17/2000

Praise The Lord!

BY WHOM

By whom were you called? By whom were you anointed or by whom were you appointed? Some human beings are called by other spirits, other than God. Some are appointed not anointed by God, by whom the seven son of Sceva was appointed. Simmon was appointed but not by God. Satan has supernatural powers. By whom did he get those powers from? Was he call, appointed or anointed? By whom, for He was created holy? He was in God's presents daily, until he rebelled. By whom did he deceive a third of the angels? They are still working for the devil today. They are still working for old Lucifer. By whom shall you be protected? By God Almighty, for he sent Jesus Christ to save the world.

04/15/2000

TITLES OF ENCOURAGEMENT

The Work of the Lord The Setting of the Sun
The Lord Is Alive and He Is dancing within My Soul
As I Pen This Letter, in This Book, It's Only through the Penmanship of the Lord The Lord with the Flag
Be Somebody and Stop Being Nobody
He Love You, Love Him Back By Finding Him

04/16/2000

Walter J. Miller

WHAT A FRIEND

I can recall the times when I didn't have food to eat, clothes to wear nor shoes to put on my feet. I went to my family and some of my so call friends. They were not able to help me. They close their doors in my face. They turned their backs on me. Out of all my trust in them, they refused to help me. I went to my Friend that I had left behind. He was a friend that I had betrayed, for my family and friends. I cried as I went without, knowing that my family and friends would care for me in my hard times. I was wrong. They betrayed me. They didn't care. I was a shame to go back to my Friend that I had left and betrayed for my family and friends. My family and friends are still doing the same thing to others as they did to me. I finally went back to my Friend. By the way, He is my best friend. He sheltered me, gave me food, clothes and helped me in my trials and tribulation. My Friend welcomed me back with open arms and forgave me all my past wrongs. That friend is Jesus, my Christ, my Lord, and my Savior. He is everything to me. He gave me a new song to sing. Every day I praise my Lord, in the name of Jesus. Now, as I pass by, my family and friends look with awe. They don't know that everything that happened to me God did it. What a friend I have in Jesus. What a friend!

04/19/2000

Be unto me as I am unto you, in Jesus name

PAUL VS PAUL

Each one of these guys had a job to do. That job was to warn the people. Saul was, also known as, Paul from Macedonia. Paul really had a job to do for he was a destroyer of God's people. The other Paul was from America. His job was to look out for the people. He had to warn them when the enemy was coming or they would perish. Saul was an enemy of the people until God changed him. God blinded him from the world and made
him a servant of His. Then, he had the job of warning the people about the forgiving grace of God. God forgave him of all his past. Paul spread the gospel all over Asia. Would you be willing to do the job of these Paul's? Would you warn the people about the love of God? How loving and forgiving He is. Be a Paul of today and warn the people. Let them know that God can and will change them the same way He did Paul. If it takes being blinded by his mighty light, so be it. Well, I must say, that both Paul's did their job. Because of the work they did, people are still being save today through the grace of God. I must become a worker for the Lord. I can warn the people of God's love and mercy. There are a lot of people who still need to be warned. Are you willing to work for God? You can let them know about God's Saving Grace. Be a Pauline of today's world.

04/26/2000

Walter J. Miller

WHO TOOK BARABBAS PLACE?

Born into sin and continued in all kinds of crimes, he was caught and was doom to die. That man name was Barabbas. There was another man. His name was Jesus. He was free of sin. Even though He was born in a world of sin, no one could find a fault in Him. The governor wanted Barabbas dead for his crimes, yet he was spared by a man who would come and take his place. Not only would he come and take his place but everyone else place in the whole world. What a man! This man name is Jesus. My brothers and sisters, would you die for somebody else? Who would you rather have died for you, Barabbas or Jesus? Would you have taken Barabbas place or Jesus? Jesus came and died for the world when he took Barabbas place. Wonder did he thank Him? Did you thank Him for taken your place on the cross, as he did for Barabbas?

04/26/2000

Because of the Blood of Jesus, I live. I will praise his name and worship Him forever

TOUCH ME

O'God, touch the hem of my garment. I am not worthy that you should touch me with thy hand. Just touch the hem of my garment so I may be made whole and be healed. O'God, touch me. Touch me at night and touch me in the daytime so that I will know that you are still close to me. Touch me until I am clean. Hallelujah! Hallelujah! Touch me Lord, for you are the lamp unto my feet. Eli, Eli, Sabachthani? Don't forsake me forever. O'Lord, touch me. I declare the light of Jesus; therefore, I shall not walk in darkness. I shall fellowship in His love and mercy for His blood covers me. Touch me!

04/30/2000

SPARE NOT

Spare not! Don't spare open rebuke because you are only sparing true love. Spare not His trials and tribulation. Spare not worrying about what tomorrow will bring. Spare not thyself from the Lord. He did not spare himself from the cross. Spare not thyself from Jesus. Repent! Repent! Spare Not!

04/30/2000

Walter J. Miller

BEING THANKFUL (For God's Help)

Dear God,

I thank you for the detour of my footsteps when I was heading in the wrong direction. I knew that I was destining for darkness. O'God, I thank your mighty angels for guiding me
in my ups and downs. I thank them for leading me to the path or righteousness. The Lord is good and His love is forever. Keep me strong, O'God, for I am weak without you. O'Lord, my enemy will devour me and cause me to fall into their pit. Father God, I thank you for being my Good Shepherd. I am one lost sheep without the Lord. I know I have a lot of thorns in my life that have to be removed. I have travel on rough pastures in my life. Please be patient with me, O'Lord. I know that Jesus will lead me to greener pastures, in your name. Job didn't have the patience that you have nor did Solomon have the love you have. Your love is the greatest. I love your ways, O'Lord. Teach me thy ways. I thank you, O'God, for all the help you give me daily. I thank you for watching over me and sheltering me from the storms. O'Lord, you are my protector, I thank you, O'God, in the name of Jesus. Amen.

04/30/2000

THE RIGHTS FOR THE WRONGS

In your life time, have you given up good for the bad or given up your rights for the wrong? Life will make you do a lot of things that you would not want to do. If a person have a right to live but instead give their life for someone else, would you call that person a hero, a savior or a donor? How did the people receive him? Did they thank him for such a precious and eternal gift? Would you praise a person like that forever? Let's keep His sacrifice alive by giving up or wrongs for the rights. Jesus died so that you can be with him forever. Will it be wrong for you to give up the world for Him? Do you think that would be right? Would you do the opposite?

05/03/2000

God is Omnipotent, having all powers...God is Omniscient, He is all knowing...
Omnipresent, He is everywhere...

Walter J. Miller

CHANGED

I once was a dog living like a hog. I use to lick my own vomit and wallow in the mud. Every time my God would help me clean myself up, I would go back to doing the same thing; rolling around in that same old "sinful pen". I use to think I was curse by my God for not doing his will. By turning back after he had cleanse me, He allowed me to lie in the mud once again and to eat of my own vomit. I cried out, "O' Lord, my God, take me out of this lot. O'Lord, change me and make me anew." I prayed day and night for that change to be wash clean of that mud and not to return to that vomit. I cried and prayed, "O'Lord, here I am. I am that I am, your child. Help me Father, in the name of Jesus, change me." One day I walked out of the mud and away from my vomit. He cleansed me and changed me. I became like an owl, real wise. I look around today and tried to help my brother and sisters to stop being that dog and that hog. Ask God for that change. He changed me and He will change you.

5/03/2000

SAVING GRACE

I am out of the cracks, from under the rocks to stand on solid ground, all by the Lord and my Savior, Jesus Christ. My spirit is free through Him. He died for my sins so that I can have life more abundantly. He is my salvation. My God came and rescued me from darkness. Now that He is my light, I will praise him all day long. My Lord redeemed me and I know that I have been changed. My God forgave me of all my past sins and made me a new creation unto him. My saving grace is Jesus. He healed all my afflictions and took away my addiction. I thank Him for he has been so good to me. Jesus is the answer. He is your saving grace.

O'Father, don't let me stray away from you so far that I can't hold your hand. Allow me to stay close enough so that I can touch the hem of your garment.

05/12/2000

Walter J. Miller

FALSE SHEPHERDS

False Shepherds come dressed to kill. Yes! They came to kill all of the weak lambs. They come to destroy all the sheep that are wounded and poor. They are worse than the real wolf. They search and destroy with bold in their eyes. They pretend to love and give care for the sheep but they won't lay down their life for the sheep. All they want to do is betray them and lead them astray. They want to mislead all of God's elect. There is only one true shepherd and that is Jesus. He is the Good Shepherd. Jesus will lay down his life for his sheep and his elect. He will not leave them alone or lead them astray. He will keep them in green pasture and they won't have to be afraid. The Lord will watch over them for he is the Good Shepherd not the False Shepherd.

05/14/2000

DON'T ASK! JUST OBEY!

Why so long, O'Lord, before you open up my eyes unto your ways? Why so long before you showed me your Glory or is it that I waited so long to believe your wisdom, knowledge and understanding. Why do I question you, O'Lord?

05/14/2000

I WILL

"I will" is a very determine phrase with plenty of power and thought, "I will" means to either succumb to that will or you live it out. It means that you heed or obey to the cause. I will serve the Lord or serve the devil. I will make up my mind. "I will" is a very powerful saying. Remember Satan, a perfect created being, he said those very words. He said, "I will ascend unto the heaven and be like the Almighty". He, also, said, "I will sit upon God's throne". Yes, my brothers and sisters, saying things into today's world means a lot. But for me, I will say that I will serve Jesus. He is my Lord and Savior. Yes, I will serve the Lord from which come my help and my strength. I will obey my God and give ear unto His word. Because we need to be ready when Jesus comes, I will.

05/15/2000

My brothers and sisters, I can still hear John crying in the wilderness, saying repent and be baptized, in the name of Jesus. Prepare your way for the Lord, give up sinful ways and repent unto the Lord for his kingdom is near.

Walter J. Miller

GOD (Of The Four Winds)

God of the four winds and the four winds as my witness, I am at peace within myself. My spirit is overly joy. I am free and I feel good. God knows I do. I have never felt this good within my spirit, with the help of the God of the four winds. I am thankful. I will praise Him, with the four winds, all day long. He is the God of the four winds. In the name of Jesus, let the God of the four winds guide your life. Let Him blow the breath of the four winds into your life. The angels are in those winds. Humble yourself to the God of the four winds. You will have peace and blessing from the God of the four winds.

05/18/2000

A LETTER TO MY DARLIN'

Dear Darlin',

As I lay here next to you with your hair glittering in the moonlight, your body look like it has been sprinkle with dust of diamond and gold. With the glow of stars in your eyes, I can just melt myself over your lovely body. With a climax rocking my whole body, I wish this feeling will last forever. Just to look at your body glowing in the night gets me so excited. I can scream out your name. This fire I hope will keep this flame burning. Darlin', when we are apart I don't feel the same. O'Darlin', honey, love me forever. I will never leave you for nothing in the world. Because I love you, I love you more than words can say. If, you only knew how much that I love you.

05/19/2000

Keep on loving me, my Darlin'

GOD'S MY PROTECTOR

I go to the Lord for safety and remain in his care for He is my defender. I trust in God. He keeps me from all hidden dangers and all deadly diseases. I need not fear of sudden attacks during the night nor do I worry about the evils that kill in the daytime. Many may fall by my side and the wicked are punished but I am not harm. The Most High is my protector. No violence will come near my house. God has put all his angels in charge of me and my household. My God protects me wherever I may go. God keeps me from disaster, when I am in trouble He comes and rescues me. I acknowledge my Lord's every word and He rewards me with long life. I will sing and honor the Lord, my God, and every day. He is supreme forever.

05/21/2000

To the sender of the winds, all the rains and thunder unto me

Walter J. Miller

A LOVING MOTHER

A loving mother is a woman of virtue. She has been blessed by God. She is a woman that keeps her husband happy. A loving mother keeps her children with a smile. She is their doctor, as well as, their nurse. A loving mother has a healing smile and a comforting touch. A loving mother is every man's dream. A loving mother will work her fingers to the bone. She will keep food on their table, clothes on their backs and shoes on their feet. Her children obey her every command. Her husband gets all his strength from her. God has blessed her abundantly. Give her flowers while she yet lives. Tell a loving mother that she is loved. A loving mother gets all of her strength from God. He gives her wisdom, knowledge and understanding to guide her family. Think how that loving mother stayed up when you were sick. Think of how she worried when you were in trouble or not around. A loving mother prays to God to protect her family when they are out of her eye sight. Her family gives thanks unto God for a loving mother.

05/26/2000

PASSING BY

This old world keeps passing by. As the sun goes down and the moon comes up, another day has come and gone. Time is passing by. People are born and they are dying. This old world keeps on passing by. Don't let your life keep passing by without the Lord. People may go and people may come but the Lord is forever. Everything may pass away but the Word of the Lord will last forever. My God lives. As long as I hold onto his Word, I will live forever. Let the world go passing by; however, don't let God and his Word go passing by. If you let him go by in this world, He will let you go passing by in the next.

05/31/2000

I want to be ready when Jesus returns. What about you?

Walter J. Miller

I TOLD AN ANGEL

I told an angel that I was lonely and he made me happy. I told an angel that I was hurt and he healed my wounds.
I told an angel that I was lost and he helped me found my way.
I told an angel about my god and he showed me his God.
I told an angel that I was hungry and he fed me.
I told an angel that I was thirsty and he gave me a drink
I told an angel that I was naked and he clothes me.
I told an angel that I was weak and he strengthened me.
I told an angel all my troubles and he solved them.
If you tell an angel all your troubles, he will carry them to God. The angels work for God. Tell him to protect you. It all comes from God. Tell an angel all your needs. God will send his angels to help you. I told an angel to listen to my prayers and to walk with me as I try to serve the Lord.
I told an angel thank you. I told an angel.

06/02/2000

Let no weapon form against you. Tell an angel all about it and he will take it to God.

THE STAGE

The stage was set two thousand years ago, when the world was void. The stage was set when God said, "Let it be" and it was. There was no scam when He said it was good. To have a stage you must have a platform and that platform was the Bible. The Bible is one book that has many books and numerous writers. They wrote all about this one Book and its one God. This God was director and producer of this book through his prophets and his servants. They wrote of his creation and commandment. Most of all, they wrote of his love for his people. He sat the stage in the way his people must act and the laws they must follow. These laws were given to them by his servant Moses. These laws were to show how much man love God, by obeying these laws. For these laws were to be put around their necks, in their hearts and minds forever. The stage was set when they disobeyed God. Until man said, "I will", the stage was set for the coming of man's sin. The stage was set for the forgiveness of those who disobeyed God. Men would receive God's grace through his only begotten Son. The stage was set for his Son to come and die for man's sins. If only you would believe Him. The stage for every man is set before God, Satan's stage is set before him and so were Adam and Eve. There were many servants who had their stage set before God; Abraham, Isaac, Jacob, Joseph, Mary, Martha and, Israel, the Egyptian, the Hebrews and any more. From the beginning of time the stage was sat, even before some was born. Let God set the stage and direct your life. He knew how you would act or what you will be before you were created. The world is God's stage. He sat it in order. We only play a part in it. We can get our reward if we obey His scriptures of the Bible. Don't let the devil set the stage for you. Leave it to God, let Him set the stage. *In the beginning God created the heaven and the earth.*

Walter J. Miller

Without Him there was nothing made.

06/04/2000

THROUGH CHRIST

Through Christ I can do everything and without Him I can't do anything. Through Christ I was saved from my addiction. Through Christ I am free. Free from my sin. Through Christ my void was filled.
Through Christ is where all my strength and help comes from. Through Christ every man, woman, boy and girl can be free. Through Christ man was given a second chance. Through Christ man can live forever.
I was dead but through Christ I live. Everybody should live their life through Christ. Through Christ man can receive salvation.
Through Christ man will be judged. Through Christ.

06/04/2000

Be not dismayed of things of this world for through Christ everything is possible. For the name of Jesus,
have faith in your everyday works.

CRY NO MORE

I cried unto my God for many years, begging Him to heal me. The affliction of lust was too much to bare. I asked Him to remove my addiction and destroy these sinful ways that are carrying me to my grave and keeping me away from my God. I will cry no more, if only, He will heal me. I pray daily asking my God o change me. At night my pillow is wet from my tears crying to my God for forgiveness. "Enough! Enough!", said the Lord, "Cry no more for I have heard your cry". "Cry no more for I am with you." "Let thyself be removed from thy ways", said the Lord, "CRY NO MORE!" I am now fifty two years old and it's His will that I am alive. There must be work we have to do. My Lord and I are on a mission. I cry no more for I have a smile and I got peace within. I am happy all day long because I see how loving my God is. I am happy where He brought me from. O'Father, I thank you for drying my tears and keeping me under your wings. I feel good that I have faith in Jesus Christ, my savior. There are times when I get weak, however, I prayed to my God for strength. Walking with Jesus is all I need, CRY NO MORE.

06/07/2000

Walter J. Miller

GOD IS GOOD

I was fellowshipping and talking with a brother the other day and when he was leaving he said, "God is good". I responded by saying, "Yes, every day. Every day that He wakes you up He is good." Then I began to think, what happens when we don't wake up? Well, I had to give that a lot of thought. When we don't wake up, maybe, it was His plan. Maybe, He'd rather take us with him than see us suffer. Maybe, our work is finish. Then, He calls us home to be with him. Sometimes, He tells us to hold on a change is coming. God is good because He helps us to bare the burdens that are too heavy for us. God is good because He will never leave us alone. Whether it rains or storms, He is good. He gives us shelter. He is good. When we go through our trials and tribulations, He hides us under his wings. That's why God is good. I know God is good for myself because I held on and He changed me. God is good for He forgave me all my sins. Today I am thankful, for my life has a new meaning. I am a new creation in His sight. I am free and I have peace in my life. Without God none of this was possible. God is good so, praise and worship Him. God is Good!

06/08/2000

UNTO YOU

Unto you, O'Lord, I put my trust for you are worthy. I am so glad I found you in time and I thank you for changing my life. Unto you, I will praise and worship you the rest of my life. Unto you, my Lord, I honor your name. I have been truly changed, redeemed by the blood of Jesus. I have a few more wounds to heal and I know that you would take care of them. Unto you, my salvation is everlasting. Your love is forever. Unto you, my life is anchored. Unto you, I call upon your name. All of my sorrows, pain and troubles, I bring unto you. Unto you, I know that I am safe and I will not be afraid. I have nothing to fear for you are with me. Unto you, I am thankful for your desire to change my life. It was impossible without you. Unto you, I am free and have peace within. You have been good to me. I want my brothers and sisters to know, unto you, they are safe. They must repent unto you.

06/12/2000

Walter J. Miller

SPIRITS

Spirits are something unseen, yet they are touching and beholding. Spirits can enlighten or darken your soul. They can tie you down. Spirits are within your soul. They can guide you and they can deceive you. Spirits are very deceptive. They are good and bad. Sometimes, it all depends on the person. Spirits follow after its kind. Spirits can harm and protect. Spirits has many forms. There is only one true spirit. That spirit is God. God manifested his Spirit in Jesus and our Lord and Savior manifested his Spirit in us. God and his Son is a pure Spirit. Spirits comes in many shapes and sizes. Spirits comes from its maker. Good spirits or evil spirits, they are spirits. The spirits are with you as you walk toward God in the Spirit of Jesus. Hear me, my brothers and sisters; listen to what the Spirit is saying to the churches. Fruits of the Spirit are a turban and a necklace unto man. God gave mankind His image which is his Spirit. Fret not thyself with evil spirits my brothers. Trust in Jesus for He controls all spirits.

06/16/2000

I OVERCAME

I look back and wonder how I overcame the evil forces of this world. I was not fighting against flesh and blood but against principalities. I overcame by the powers of God and depending on Jesus. It was all God's doing. He gave His only begotten Son so that I can have life more abundantly. I thank you Jesus for the sacrifice of your blood by dying on the cross. Your blood saved me and I overcame the evil forces of this world. Your name gave me the strength to overcome and I overcame the sins of the world. Father God, I thank you for taking this thorn out of my side. Once in my life I can say I have truly overcome. I overcame, I overcame, in the name of Jesus, I overcame.

06/22/2000

THANKFUL

Father God, I thank you for traveling up and down the highways with me, Elouise, Almando and Elijah. I thank you for watching over us from day to night. You returned us safe in one piece, with one mind, one soul and one spirit. In the name of Jesus, I thank you. There's no one who could have made this possible but you, O'Lord. The angels obeyed your every command by watching over us.

06/22/2000

Walter J. Miller

MY STRENGTH

Knowing that I have God and all His angels by my side, whom shall I fear? My strength comes from the Lord and Savior, Jesus Christ. God is good and His love and mercy is everlasting. Blessed is the man that put his trust in the Lord. I have no strength, if I don't have God. I have faith in his word when he said he will never leave me. My strength keeps my faith in Jesus. Daily as I walk toward him, I fall weak sometimes. I ask my God to strengthen me and make me strong again. Keep me strong O'Lord, in your name for you are my strength.

06/24/2000

Blessed is the man that has God as a friend. Repent unto God for your sins and be forgiven, in Jesus name. Amen

THE SEA (Sailing)

From the sea I came ashore to anchor myself in this harbor, to dock at this pier. I came to roam the seashore. I came to seek rest from the storms of life. The sea was rough and the waves were tough but my God came and calm the sea. He saw that I made it safely to the shore. I dock at His port where I praised his name. He said he will never leave me. This world can be a sea. The trials and tribulations you go through can be the waves or the storms. The Lord will let you go sailing through them. That's when you dock and anchor yourself to Jesus. God has brought you safely ashore. Jesus can and will calm all storms in your life. He is your bridge over trouble waters and the shelter in the storms. If you go to sea sailing, let God and Jesus be your captain and co-captain.

06/25/2000

Walter J. Miller

TRIALS

We go through trials every day, to see how much we can bare but most of all to see how strong our minds are. For, if our minds are weak then we are weak. Sometimes, we pretend to have a powerful mind but our thoughts are weak. Mind power is a vital part of your everyday activeness. Therefore you have to rely on something or someone greater than yourself. I can relate to this because there are factors that you go through in your thinking. You need a strong will or a strong factor that you can rely on. Some people are born with certain elements that can carry them through, if not, they are taught how to handle their trials. If you can't handle those trials in life then there's only one who is greater than all. That's the Almighty. He gives freely what you need or ask for. He is the maker of wisdom, knowledge and understanding. These trials are all part of our life but with the help of the Lord we can make it. As I look over my trials, I could not have made it without the Lord. My brothers and sisters, take Jesus to trial with you. Let Him speak for you, in his name everything will be alright.

06/26/2000

BROKEN PROMISES

As I go over these vows to look at the broken promises, I wanted to see how they occur and why they were broken. Even, the saints and the elect broke these promises. Why? Temptation, lust of the flesh, greed, power, and material things; these things cause an invisible ring and broken promises to appear. They lose the spirit which was giving them. Their minds get short and their arms and eyes get long. They forget their promise of love, honor and obey. These are human being and unproductive creature that God has made. They even broke their promise to their maker. Human being makes vows and promises to one another. There promises are not like God's great promise when He promises to never leave us. These promises are spoken and broken freely in our way of life daily. These human beings see each other face to face and know their worth. How can you say that you love the Lord whom you can't see face to face? I once was part of that broken promise but something happened. God changed my life. I made Him this promise. If He will take away my addiction and forgive me of all my sins, I promised to serve Him. Then, I ask Him to show me what love really was. I wanted to know. I wanted to promise to love Him. I wanted to know what it meant to love, honor and obey until death we do part. How many times some of us have died, yet we live? God kept his promise when He said that He will send us a Savior. Man can be a savior to a woman or a woman to a man. With the help of God there will be no broken promise. The ring will not be broken when we put our trust in Him. Sometimes, promises are broken. We go through our trials and tribulation trying to keep these promises. Sometimes, we go through things God has already predestined for us, in that case our promises are void. My brothers and sisters don't make or take a vow and let it become a broken promise.

Walter J. Miller

06/27/2000

WHAT THE LORD HAS DONE FOR ME

That what the Lord has done for me, I am going to do it unto my brothers and sisters. He worked for me and now that I am a new creation, I must work for the Lord. I am going to spread His word all over this land, to every living thing, even the birds of air. I am going to fellowship with my brothers and sisters and help bare their burdens, in the name of Jesus. What the Lord has done for me? He has blessed me abundantly by redeeming me. What the Lord has done for me, no man has never attempted to do. There were times when I was in jail. Even though, I was locked up, I had faith in the Lord. I was free in body, mind and spirit because the Lord was with me. What the Lord has done for me, I can never repay Him. He shed His blood by dying on the cross. That's what the Lord has done for me. Be not dismayed with what the Lord will and can do for you, if, you would turn to Him. What the Lord has done for me? He has given me a new song to sing. He has given me a new way of life, in my thinking, talking and walking. I can't say enough of what the Lord has done for me. I must give Him all the Glory for He has given me the victory. That's what the Lord has done for me!

06/28/2000

No weapon will form against me in Jesus name.

FOR JESUS SAKE

I sit here wondering about my past, thinking how good it feels now that God has my life. I am free and I have peace within myself. I am happy about this Spirit that my God has bestowed upon me. It was all for Jesus sake. I never had it so good! With the Lord, I have a sound mind and a clean heart. It's all for Jesus sake. I want to serve God for Jesus sake. I am so happy with what God has done for me for Jesus sake. I am very thankful. I call Jesus, Jesus, Jesus, for Jesus sake. I am healed and I can say Amen and Amen. God is great and His love is forever. I know that everything works for the Glory of God. It's all for Jesus sake.

06/29/2000

I am an Overcomer of this world for Jesus sake

Walter J. Miller

GOING THROUGH

As I'm going through my redeem life, which the Almighty changed, I am very grateful. I thank Him daily for that change. There are many more areas I need help in for what I am going through. I need strength in my walk and my talk because Satan is still up to his same old tricks. I pray daily to my Lord God and Savior, Jesus Christ to help me. I know that He will stand by me in the things I am going through. I am, yet, a babe in His eyesight. I am still crawling and I need a lot of milk and nursing. Maybe one day I will be able to receive solid food that will make me strong. I want to be strong enough to handle the things that I am going through, I want to be able to help my brothers and sisters carry on to Jesus. I want to be able to pray with them when they are going through. Even though, I will be able to walk and talk on my own, I still will need Jesus hand to guide me. When I am going through, He will be there for me. I will need His love to keep me steady and strong, when I am going through, He will let no weapon form against me prosper. I will have on His whole armor to protect me when I am going through.

06/29/2000

I am an Overcomer of this world through the Blood of Jesus. Amen.

THAT SMALL! HOW LITTLE!

The size of a mustard seed, it's that small, how little being patient with a little bit of faith goes a long way. With a little love that small, how little it will hurt, just to give yourself over to a peaceful situation. All it takes is a little care that small, how little. Sometimes, when you get angry and things don't go your way as plan, that's when tempers flares. All you have to do is have a little patient the size of a mustard seed, that small, how little. Stop the anger and the violence will go away. Just show a little love, that small, how little it will take to make a person smile or save some one life. That small, how little the size of a mustard seed. Jesus said these very words. Why not obey Him, not them. They are His words that small, how little.

06/30/2000

Walter J. Miller

MY EYES HAVE SEEN

My eyes have seen His Glory. For, He showed me victory when I was defeated. I have felt His power. The coming of the Lord is going to be great. No more sin and no more pain. Everyone and everything is going to be under His control. My eyes have seen many trouble days. My eyes have not seen the righteous forsaken or begging for bread. My eyes have seen so much sin. I, myself, have committed so much sin. I wonder why my eyes have seen so much. Even the righteous go bad and the unrighteous do good. My eyes have seen a loving and merciful God. He is a God of no respecter person. My eyes has seen Him love the righteous, as well as, the unrighteous. He wants the sinful ones in His care so they can return unto Him with a repented heart. My eyes are waiting on my Savior, the Lord Jesus Christ to come again. My eyes are sat on the coming of the Lord. Then, my eyes have seen.

07/02/2000

Pray ye for one another, for the day of the Lord is near

FILLED TO THE BRIM

O' what mercy my God has shown me! I once was empty. To the word of my Lord and Savior, Jesus Christ, I prayed. He filled this void in my life with His word. He filled my life to the brim of how to love my brothers and sisters. I have peace in my life now and it's filled to the brim. I am filled to the brim with His wisdom, knowledge and understanding. Empty no more because I am filled to the brim with joy. I am filled to the brim with Jesus. Thank God for I am filled to the brim.

07/06/2000

A man spirit will rise no higher than what he thinketh.

FRET NOT

Fret not of the things of this world. The Lord is with thee. I fret not of you loving me. If not for your love I would be lost. I fret not of my evil doers for they shall meet God. In the name of Jesus, I fret not. The mercy and goodness of God is everlasting. I fret not for He gave His only begotten Son for me so that I can have life more abundantly. I fret not for the coming of the Lord for I am ready and waiting on the Lord. I want to see His Glory and receive my crown. I have run a good race of faith. I fret not of being a servant of the Lord; it is good unto my soul. Fret not for what your fellowman can do for you, but what you can do for your fellowman. Fret not thyself of what you can do for God for He can do all things. So, depend on God and fret not.

07/06/2000

When you get wisdom, knowledge and understanding, you have God.

Walter J. Miller

TEARS OF FEAR

I went through many trials and tribulations. I have seen many trouble days and had plenty of sleepless nights. I have seen many of my friends and foes come and go. Many are in tears of fear, because they have not yet found peace in their life. Many would perish from lack of knowledge. They face those tears of fear because they have not repented unto their God or known the true God. By knowing Him, He would have dried those tears of fear. All those tears of fear would have been done away with. All you have to do is depend on Him. Then, there will be no more tears of fear. The only fear you should have is the fear of God. And then there would be no more tears of fear. They would be all wiped away. There will only be tears of joy and the fear of the Lord. Carry all those tears of fear to the Lord. That would end all of your Tears of Fear.

07/08/2000

Fear the Lord my brothers and sisters and live.

VICTORY

I was a sinner most of my life. My God came and rescued me. He pulled me out of the fire. My adversary had me thinking that I was dead in sin and I will never be raise up unto God. Even though I have many areas in my life that need cleansing, I received Victory through my God. I did not know my loving God. He gave His only begotten Son as a ransom so that I can have life. What a God! What a ransom, for me. My sins had me believing that there was no hope. Through Jesus there is hope. My sins kept me apart from God. I did not have the powers that other believers had. I was a shame to call on the name of Jesus. I did not want to face the days ahead for my sins had me down. Through the grace of God, I have salvation. By Jesus dying on the cross, I have victory. With Jesus walking and talking to me daily, I can feel that victory. With the angels He has placed around me, I am assured victory. I can face all temptation along with my adversary. I am liberated through Jesus Christ, my Lord and Savior. I am depending on Jesus. With His power, I know day to day, he will lead me to victory. He will protect me daily as I face this sinful world. Lord, I thank you for being my Lord. There is no other name I can receive victory from. I pray, O'Lord, help me kick all these bad habits that's not becoming of you. I know that they will hinder me from receiving my victory. As I run this race of faith and hold onto your hand, you will give me Victory.

07/16/2000

Walter J. Miller

FLOWERS OF THORNS

Flowers of thorns are a thing to see. If you see them standing in the bi-ways or highways, keep on riding or walking. Some are destitute, some are infidels and some you can't resist their smell. Flowers of thorns, O' how they can scorn by their touch. You would curse the day you were born. These flowers of thorns are full of deceit. They never say no to a change. Flowers of thorns are deep rooted in their ways. This can be very deep, death do they heap. As a friend I say do not keep. Flowers of thorns, don't misbehave with them. For they will send you to your grave. These flowers are wild; however, they can be transplanted and nourished by the word of God. He shall tame their seed. Blessed be the name of the Lord Jesus. He is the Savior for the Flowers of Thorns.

07/22/2000

FIGHT FOR FREEDOM

A fight for freedom is a fight to be free. This means you have to know what you are fighting for. Sometimes a fight doesn't have to be physical, but mental. Sometimes that's harder than fighting physically. Fighting a fight for freedom with the mind can be even tiresome. It's even harder with the flesh. You fight for freedom to get out of bondage, for this flesh have you in prison, in the body. Sometimes a fight for freedom can get out of hand. That's when you put your trust in someone hand that is bigger than yours. That hand is the hand of God, the Lord Almighty. Through our Lord Jesus Christ, our fight for freedom was done. He is our Savior. He not only fought for our freedom, he died for our freedom. God gave us our freedom by giving His only begotten Son. That was our salvation. All we have to do is believe God will fight for our freedom.

08/01/2000

Walter J. Miller

THE LAW OF THE LORD

The law of the Lord, it's your defender against the wicked.
The law of the Lord has healing, safety, justice and love.
The law of the Lord has values.
Devote yourself to the Lord. The proud don't obey the law of the Lord. They dig traps for those who do. Obey the law of the Lord. It's sweeter than honey unto your soul. Follow the instruction of the law of the Lord and keep its command for it's a light unto thy feet. Let it be your guide and desire with dedication for the law of the Lord. Be faithful and don't neglect the law of the Lord.

08/29/2000

I look unto the hill from where all my help comes from.

PRAISE

When you praise the Lord, He will praise you. When you walk with Jesus, He will walk with you.
When you look unto the Lord, He will look unto you.
Let all His mercy and kindness be yours. When you seek the Lord, He will seek you.
Praise Him daily for He is worthy of all your Praise.

08/29/2000

THE BIBLE

The Bible is a light unto my feet for it nourish my soul. The days of old were when my forefathers and my father looked to the Bible for their guide. The Bible is your defender in times of trouble. It is a light in dark times and will lead you to safety. The Bible is a doctrine of the true Divine, His revelation unto the world. The Bible gives me wisdom, knowledge and understanding. It comforts me in my trials and tribulation. Read the Bible. There are no secrets about it untold. Live the Bible. Its light will shine before man. The Bible tells us how to love one another and teach us healing. There are no other documents of God other than the Bible.

09/01/2000

A VOW

I_____, accept Jesus as my personal Savior to be Lord over my life. I come before you just as I am. I am sorry for my sins. I repent of all my sins and ask you to forgive me, in Jesus name. I shall follow you every day of my life. Come, Lord Jesus, into my life and save me and heal me. Amen.

09/14/2000

Mission of the Goodshepherd, Inc.

Walter J. Miller

IN MY CASE

In my case, when I was going through my trials and tribulation, my God was there. In my case, there was times that my God would talk to me because of the wrongs I had hanging over my head. In my case, I thought He had left me and would not hear my cry and listen to my prayer but I was wrong. In my case, I never knew that my God love me so. In my case, I always had respect for my God, praising Him, doing His will and understanding His revelation. In my case, that's how I made it this far. In my case, I am walking and talking with Jesus. In that case, I am going to keep on serving the Lord. In my case.

09/21/2000

MORTAL MAN

Mortal man, God have chosen you to watch over His flock. Mortal man, you were created lower than the angel. You were created in His image. This mean you are next to God in spirit. Mortal man, you are responsible for His sheep; to take care of them to heal all the wounded and to search for all the ones that are lost. Mortal man, you are to bound up all their wounds and feed them mentally, physically and spiritually. Mortal man, God have anointed you to lead and teach His sheep. Mortal man, you are to lead them in greener pastures. Mortal man, you are to guide them in the right direction. You are their shepherd and they are your sheep. Mortal man, God have given you a load to carry. Just obey Him and He will help you carry that load. Mortal man, the Lord would not put any more on you than you can carry. Be strong for the Lord is with you, Mortal man. Mortal man, He will never leave you or forsake you, in the name of Jesus. Mortal man, God loves you. You were made for Jesus, Mortal man.

09/26/2000

Walter J. Miller

PRAYER

I am the greater for I am in Him that's in me; therefore no weapon form against me will prosper. All my strength comes from Him. I can do all things through Him. He is my God, my Lord and my Savior, whom I believe. I am the head and not the tail. The Lord is my Shepherd, I shall not want for I am content, I have peace and I am richly blessed in His Spirit. I am an overcomer of this world, in the name of Jesus.

10/15/2000

PLEAD MY CAUSE O'LORD

O'Lord, I pray daily for you to protect and defend me against my enemy. O'Lord, help me for I am my own enemy. My sinful ways are ever before you. O'Lord, plead my cause and deliver me. Plead my cause, O'Lord, and change me. Keep me from being an enemy toward you. Plead my cause, O'Lord. I am sorry of my sin. Every day, O'Lord, plead my cause that I may walk in your ways and obey your every command. Reach out and touch my mind, my heart and cleanse me of all my wrongs. Plead my cause, O'Lord, unto my Father and His mighty angels; forgive me for I mourn all day long. For the sake of your love, Plead My Cause, O'Lord.

10/18/2000

O'ISRAEL

O'Israel! Listen unto the word of the Lord, "Let not your heart be troubled, believe in me. O'Israel, keep thy commandments and I will keep my promise. I made a promise unto your Fathers, Abraham, Isaac, Jacob and David. O'Israel, I have led you out through deep waters on dry land. I fed you with milk and honey. I was with you day and night. I guided you toward still waters. I showed you my powers by guiding you with fire at night and shading you in the day time. To show you just how much I love you, O'Israel. O'Israel, I even gave you water from the rock. Even though you turn your backs on me, I protected you with my cloud. O'Israel, O'Israel, I will never leave you. Keep my Spirit upon thyself, O'Israel. I have kept my word into thy Fathers that I will always be your Goodshepherd. O'Israel, how long will thy not hearken unto my voice? O'Israel, how long are you going to worship other gods? O'Israel, I am sending you a message by my mighty angels. O'Israel, return unto me. O'Israel!"

10/26/2000

Walter J. Miller

THAT BRILLIANT FLAME

There is a brilliant flame that shines forever. It shines in Africa, Asia, North America, South America and all over the world. This brilliant flame is in every man's heart. It is there to guide and protect him, as he goes through trials and tribulation on his way to victory. That brilliant flame first appeared in our Lord and Savior Jesus Christ. The Holy Spirit was next with a fire that burned in a man's soul. This brilliant flame is to ward off darkness. This brilliant flame watches over us daily. It burns forever and ever. Come close to this brilliant flame, it would never lead you. It will forever be by your side to guide and protect you. Jesus Christ is that Brilliant Flame.

01/05/01

WATCHING AFTER ME

Dear Lord,

I thank you for being there for me, in times of trouble. I could not find a better friend than thee to depend on. I can recall something that you told me long ago and it is still hold dear in my heart to this day. You said that you would never leave me alone and that you will always be there for me. I found out something that holds a lot of true. You will never find anything if you do not go looking for it. I thank you, in the name of Jesus, for looking after me. Your mighty angels guide me daily. They are by my side every day. They protect all the good times and bad alike. They are there for me. All I had to do was to look up and reach out. When I needed shelter and safety all I had to do was get on your wings.

01/08/01

NO MORE

No more am I a sinner, but a child of God.
No more am I the tail but the head.
No more am I the borrower but the lender.
My God has brought me up from the bottom to the top.
No more am I the dog returning to my own vomit.
No more will I cast my pearls to swine.
No more will I depend on man but I am depending on my Lord and Savior, Jesus Christ.
Jesus Christ died for me and my sins. I am very grateful. I will praise Him forever and worship Him all day long.
No more will I have to go to man for help.
My God has redeemed me and I know I have been change.
No more will I cry unto my Lord and He will not hear my cry.
No more my Brothers.
No more my Sisters.
You would have to shed a tear in vain no more. Just call his name and have faith that He is coming back. Death will be no more. Pain and sickness would be no more.
Darkness will be no more.

01/08/01

AN ECHO

Yes! I can, also, hear Jehovah crying saying, "Repent, repent and be baptized, in the name of Jesus." Prepare your way for the Lord for He is coming back. Let us come off that old dreadful road of sin. Repent for His kingdom is near. Can't you hear His voice calling?

01/09/2001

LOVING THE LORD

My brothers and sisters, there is no one better you can love than loving the Lord. His grace and mercy are forever. He said, "Love as I have loved you." So, brothers, in this world love the Lord. He will love you. Whether you love Him or not, He will always love you. Even if you leave Him, He will never leave you. Be servants of the Lord by loving your brothers and sisters in spirit and in truth. That's LOVING THE LORD.

01/09/2001

I AM NOT WORTHY

Oh! Father, I am not worthy to even call your name. When I was a babe, out of my mother's womb, you came and saved me. You wiped all the filth away from me and cut my navel cord. You bathe me in salt and ripped your garment in pieces to wrap me in. I was a bloody mess and you nursed me day after day. You sat me aside and you taught me many things. You even built me a house. You watched me grow daily in statute. I grew tall and handsome. You gave me a cloak to wear and a pair of sandals for my feet. You put a necklace around my neck, a crown upon my head and a gold belt around my waist. As I grew, I forgot the love that you had shown me. I forgot the things you taught me through the years, from my youth. Oh! My Father, forgive me and cover me in your blood, not mine. I am not worthy, Father. God reached out your ever loving and merciful hands and save me. Give me the love that you gave me as a child. I have repented! Oh! Father, I know that I am not worthy but only say the words that I may be healed. I am not worthy.

01/11/2001

Walter J. Miller

A SOLIDER (My Father)

A soldier is a special servant or person in warfare for a cause. That cause is to save lives, make peace and destroy your enemy. The cause can be many things. Being a soldier in the army of the Lord, we deal only with things that are not of God. We deal with things such as; sin for God is not sin. He came into this world to save the world from sin. He will send a soldier into battle to fight sin in the world. A soldier is sent on many missions, sometimes for life and sometimes for a short while. A good soldier never complained of the suffering and wounds he received because good soldiers will endure. His master is by his side and has complete trust in the soldier. The soldier will face his enemy face to face, for he has no fear of him. The Lord will uphold him in every warfare and mission he is sent on. The Master needs a soldier of courage to send on special missions; to cast out sin, to heal the sick, comfort the lowly and take care of widows. My Father was a good soldier. His Master called him home to give him another rank and an order to sit by his side. The Master picked another soldier to go into the warfare of the world. My father was a good soldier for the Lord. I love him this day for he and God gave me life. I wanted to be a good soldier like my father, for the Lord. I did not know him that well. However, the things I heard people say about him and his attitude, you never knew when he was sad.

01/12/2001

SILENT WORDS

Jazz has many silent words, yet, it can be heard all over the world. Silent words are spoken loud and clear. Silent words fill the heart and mine. Silent words carry its message to the soul and shape the body. Silent words heal all wounds and mend broken hearts. Silent words turn frowns around.

Silent words replace love where there was once hate. Silent words talk back but are never heard. I wish my God would listen to my silent words. He was silent with silent words.

01/20/2001

On your back is a bad spot to be in, however, the good part is you are always looking up!

Walter J. Miller

G. E. D.

What does G.E.D. mean to me? God's Eternal Decision. This means He wants all of his servants to get an education so the devil won't out smart his Saints. That is why I went back to school. I went back to learn everything I could so I will be smarter than my adversary in this secular world. You have to stay on a higher level than your peers. Christian or not, you need a G.E.D. or a diploma when you're trying to strive for a better life. Yes, God can give it to you. You need to strive for a higher education to meet all your goals in this world. God would take care of you in the next. Your teachers will help you. They are not God but give them praise for they are worthy. They are chosen by God as his chief G.E.D., General Education Department. He will give them their reward.

03/01/2001

THE DEVIL MADE ME DO IT!

Yes! The devil made me do it! I know you'll remember that old saying. Well, he made me turn back to my God. He betrayed me so much, I got tired. There are other old sayings too; Lord help me and God please forgive me. I didn't want to turn to God but He told me about his son, Jesus. Someone that is stronger than the devil that would help me fight this warfare. Many times the devil would make me betray my God. For years the devil made me do it. He made me deceived my Jesus. There were times I wanted to kill myself for deceiving my Lord. But I thought about how much He loved me. When I sinned against the Holy Spirit, it convicted me. The Spirit taunted me daily for I was reminded of all my wrong doings. I prayed and prayed and asked God's forgiveness. The devil told me that God would not listen. There were times when I would believe him. Why? I don't know. All I can say is, the devil made me do it. He would tell me that God did not love me because I am a sinner. The devil is a liar. God gave his only Son for a sinner and I know He loves me. The devil wanted to destroy me before God had a chance to save me. That would place me in the devil hands forever. Thanks go to my God for sending his Son. So, my brothers and sisters don't let the devil make you do it. Choose God!

03/14/2001

Walter J. Miller

X-RAY

I know you learned that Wilhelm Roentgen invented the X-ray. They gave man the credit but it was God. He had been looking within man from the outside from the beginning of time. Man needs a machine to aid him but God need only himself. God even know how to run a MRI, not that it is amazing! God even know about physiology for He is all knowing. God is the only mind reader. He can scan your body whole just by looking at you. Can man do that? No! God gave man the ability to heal. Yes! He gave him the choice to do as he wishes. Man became selfish with his own desires. Manmade medication through the wisdom and knowledge of God, with understanding to help his brother and sister. Man became proud. God still blessed him because God had seen through man's heart. He didn't need a machine. From the beginning of time God looked into man's mine. Just as the book of Ecclesiastes states, "There is nothing new under the sun".

03/18/2001

A REVELATION

Time out for Genesis. It's time for a revelation. You have lived in the belly of the world for the word of God is against you. He knows you are trying to hide. Repent! Repent! The Lord will bring you out. The Lord is coming soon and very soon. My brothers and sisters, turn to the Lord. Have faith in the Lord for He is your salvation.

05/20/2001

LEGACY OF A LEGEND

In the beginning was the word and the word was God for the word was with God. There is nothing without the word of God for that word is the Son of God. The Savior is Jesus Christ, whom God gave for our sins.

My brothers and sisters, Jesus died for our sins on the cross. He spoke a legacy, "It is finished". It was not finished. That was the beginning of a legacy. Those same words still echo today for it was a beginning for all sinners.

Give thanks unto the Almighty God for giving his only Son to pay a debt we owed. We have a chance now to approach the throne of grace freely, in the name of Jesus. We must be like Elijah, John and so many who have prepared a way for the word. The word is coming back.

"It is Finished," was the beginning of freedom for all sinners for salvation began at the cross. Think!
The legacy of a legend.

That legend was Jesus, the only begotten Son of God. Not only does his legacy hold truth but a legend never dies.

0701/2001

Walter J. Miller

KNOWING YOUR ADVERSARY
(AKA Satan, Foes or Demons)

The Bible clearly teaches me that demons are real and they are a real problem to many Christians. I am warned to be alert because Satan is like a lion. He prowls and come roaring. I am told to put on the armor of God to fight this devil. I know of some Christians who have fallen from the church because of their adversary. I am responsible for my choices and actions that I made before God. I cannot blame the devil. I must acknowledge my own sins for I am called a child of a King. I am reminded that my adversary can do me no harm. My God told me as long as I hold onto his hand; I have the one greater in me than the one that's in the world. The Bible does not teach that all sickness or mental sickness come from my adversary or demonic attacks. I know that some sickness come from demonic results; demons that are routed to direct contact. I rest in my God's provision. I am in His care. I can remember when Paul prayed for God to remove a thorn in his flesh. God is the answer! My personal struggles are different. All of these facts must be held in contention and not forgotten. I believe the power of my God. He can best equip me for this spiritual warfare with my adversary.

07/07/2001

FAMILY AND FRIENDS DAY

As I speak on family and friend's day, I thank my God for being my friend. Not only my friend, but my Best Friend. Friends as I speak to you, let the Spirit of God guide me. Family and friends, I say we are blessed. As the old saying goes, "a family that prays together stays together". Who is there to depend on, in time of trouble, than a real good friend? Depend on the family of God, you've got a friend. I thank God for being the head of my family. With a friend like Him, you can't go wrong. So, don't let this be the last family and friend's day. It should be every day that you live. As long as you've got God, you've got a friend. There are some friends that will stand by your side closer than a brother. I found that in, Mr. and Mrs. Beasley, Mr. James and Mrs. Hellen. They welcomed me into the family with love. I thank my God for the friendship that we have, in Jesus name.

07/13/2001

MY HOPE IN THEE

The Lord said unto me and thee, "I Am That I Am". I am the way and I am the light. There is no darkness there in. I gave my only begotten Son so that you can have life. God said, "Have faith in my word for I have no lies in me." Hold onto that faith for it will guide you daily as you walk through this life. Pray unto me in faith and I will answer you; to show my love for thee and for keeping your faith in me.

08/05/2001

Walter J. Miller

UNFOLDING LOVE

Unfolding love comes from a loving source. I have a God that has this unfolding love. He loves us. Despite all the wrongs we have done, God still loves us. We as brothers and sisters should have this unfolding love. If we are to be like him, we should have an unfolding love for one another. This love does not envy, it does not hurt, and it is always forgiving. For God so loved the world that he gave us an unfolding love. He gave us his son, Jesus. I pray daily that my God will give me this unfolding love.

08/26/2001

PRAYER

I came to you O'Lord this day; lend your ear unto my prayer. O' Lord, listen unto my plea, for I am ever before thee. O' Lord, I worship and praise, as of days of ole. You said to call upon your name and you would answer. Hear me O'Lord for I am in trouble. Hear me, O'Lord, I know that thy loves me. O'Lord, you gave your only begotten son to die on the cross for my love. O'Lord, you put a hedge of your angels all around me to protect me day and night. O'Lord, your word is like a bit in a horse's mouth, they guide me daily. Those are your words unto me.

09/01/2001

THE SPIRIT

I was powerless over my addiction and the things I was weak for. I was in bondage and my sinful nature had me bound. Thanks for the love of God, he sent his only begotten Son to save me. He was born in the likeness of a simple man, who did not live in that state. The requirement of the law, by the Holy Spirit, was for my Savior to be born of the flesh. A sinful nature is hostile to God. That is why He sent his Son; to pay with his life for all sinners that were in the nature of man. Let the Spirit guide you all the days of your life.

09/01/2001

From a Friend to a Friend

Walter J. Miller

POWERS

We speak of power such as; supernatural powers, cosmetic and dark powers of this universe. These powers are not known to man. You can become hostile to God by these powers. These powers are all of darkness. They are not of God for the Lord and Savior gives all power. This power of the Lord is his and his only. No one can explain His source of power. God gave man a certain amount of power on the day of creation. These powers were given to man as a gift to rule over his domain. God gave these powers to rule the sea, the land, the animals and all creepy things. Man was made in God's own image. God gave him power through the goodness of Himself. Men began to abuse and misuse those piles. Man began to get out of control with those powers. God had to discipline man for He had all merciful power. God is all-powerful.

09/02/2001

On the day of the Lord, the Angels will rejoice, the Saints will be glad and the Demons will scream.

HIS WORD NEVER FAILS

On September 11th, 9/11, there were more fulfillment of this word; which never return void. This tragic thing that happened, the massacre of thousands of innocent people and the action of aggression, meant war against those responsible. People lives were snatched away from them. Dead or alive, my brothers and sisters, my God would never leave his word void. God said that there will be wars and rumors of wars. Just look around, open your eyes and see. Listen unto His word and never let go for his word will protect you at all times. God's word would teach you how to get around those mountains and be safe doing those trials and tribulations. Most of all have faith brother for the word was in the beginning. With God's word, you always find peace. Pray this peace. O'Father, holy is your name. Keep me safe as I walk in this land. Teach me how to love my enemies and to forgive those who hurt me.

09/11/2001

O'Father, show me your ways and let your mighty angels keep protecting me daily, in the name of your son, Jesus.

Walter J. Miller

DISASTER STRIKE

I pleaded with my brothers and sisters to find God before disasters strike. If they find God, they would find peace! Many times, when I minister to my brothers, I would ask them, "What would you do if disaster strikes"? Would they be content or would they be confused? As I look at the World Trade Center and the Pentagon, my heart goes out to all directly and indirectly involve in the rescue of the living and the dead. My heart goes out to the wounded and those that are burned. This was a time to be content for God moaned with you. He knows it all, even before it ever happened. Carry that hurt and pain to him. It's time for a healing. Pray my brother, pray my sister. Not just now but forever, in the name of Jesus pray!!! We all need him now. His words are being fulfilled day by day. That lets us know, He will be coming soon. Don't let another disaster strike without the Lord. Repent! For the time is near. When disasters strike, be with the Lord. Don't be lost when He returns. That Would Be A Disaster!

09/19/2001

I FELL DOWN

There was a time when I was always away from the Lord. I had fallen into sin. I could not stand before the devil because I was weak. I was in a circle going around and around in my sin daily. My burden was heavy and the devil had me in bondage. The people of the world had no love for me, for the world was my enemy. There is no greater love than the love of the Lord for he died for my sins. I was down, I had falling very low. I was never too low for the Lord. He reached down low and picked me up. I was dead and He redeemed my soul. I am now a living new creature unto Him for the grace of God is forever. When you find favor with the Lord, you have a good thing. The blessing of the Lord is great. I felled down but the Lord had mercy upon my soul and He healed me. Now, I am raised up unto the Lord. No man can take away from me what the Lord has done for me. There is a solid bond between Him and me. My God has anointed me to the priesthood. I want to be a priest forever for the Lord. To serve God and to be a priest of my household is my destiny. I am a minister for God and to His people.

10/07/2001

Walter J. Miller

THE ROOT OF WISDOM

The root of wisdom is God, the most high. Seek wisdom, knowledge, and understanding. Find Jesus and let him pour out his love from his root of wisdom. Fear Him in honor. Praise Him and He will give you joy. The root of wisdom is to do His will and keep His commandments. The root of wisdom has very strong branches. Its limbs will not be broken. His root is very deep. He is the root of wisdom.

08/31/2001

SO MANY THINGS

Dear Elouise,

There are so many things I have to say about why I love you. There are so many reasons that I just can't count or say them all. Honey, I can't even say how much I love you! There are so many things that get in the way. I can never say how much I love you because I would be saying I love you forever and I do. So many times, so many things remind me of you when you are not around. There are so many things I can say to make you love me. There are so many things I can say that would make you hate me, also. But me loving you as I say, I should not say anything to make you cry. You never hurt the one you love. There are so many things that make love last. However, there is only one that can make it last forever and that one is God.

12/28/2001

THE FINAL RIDE (Saddle Up)

Saddle up for this final ride. Put on your whole armor, sit tight in your saddle with your feet in your stirrup and hold tight to your reins. These horses would be galloping to the North, South, East, and West. Which horse will you saddle up? Will it be the red one or the black one, the white one or maybe the pale one? Each one has a commission of destruction to perform. Let's talk about the red horse, Revelation 6:4, who have the power and authority to make war upon the earth. Let's also look at the black horse. This rider had a pair of scales in his hands, which represent weight and measure for controlling the price of everything like barley and wheat. The price of barley and wheat was so high that the poor could not buy them. Let's go on and look at the pale horse. The rider on this horse was more destructive than the others for he had power in the four winds to kill through war, disease, starvation and famine. Which horse would you be riding? Behold! There was another horse, a white one, who in Revelation 6:2 had power to conquer. This rider was very deceptive. This rider had a bow in his hand. This rider came to deceive God's elect. Don't get caught saddling up and riding the wrong horse. Blessed be the name of God, for God so loved the world that he gave his only begotten Son. Let's not be deceived by anyone. There is only one true rider on the white horse, Revelation 19:11. The rider on this white horse had a sword in his mouth. The sword is the word of God and his word is final. His word will never return void. Let's get ready for this final ride. We are going to gird up our loin and put on the whole armor of God, which ride upon the true white horse in revelation 19:11. Read and show yourself approved. Saddle up and ride with the Lord for he is our only Savior, in the name of Jesus.
01/05/2002

Walter J. Miller

FEELING SECURITY

I feel very secure, when I found security in his love. There is peace and love under the protection of his wings. Trouble may come and trouble may go, I am very content with his love. I feel warmth of his love as He sheltered me from the storms. I may leave but I always find myself returning to that love. I found His love is always the same, never dull but sharper than a two edge sword. The security of his love would make the weak strong. My brothers and sisters, find security in God's love, where there is peace. The love of Jesus is peace. There is no other love greater than the love of God.

01/11/2002

Being secured in his love is peace

UPON HIS WORD

There are times when we are going to have to depend upon His word. For the word of the Lord is true. His word would not return void. From the beginning it was upon His word that light prevail over darkness. Even, the waters gave way to land upon His word. The whole world was created upon His word; the animals, the stars, the moon, the trees, the plants and the flowers all was create upon His word. Then upon His word, He created man after his own likeness. He, also, gave man the whole world to subdue. God gave him everything; the animals, the trees, the stars, the moon and the rivers. With all this, man was still not happy. Upon His word God made man a companion. He made a woman to comfort man, to be his help mate. God gave man all this for his love because He loved him. Upon His word, He gave man the rain and the sun. God wanted to be praise and worship, in return. There is nothing that God would not do for you, if you would obey Him. The same thing goes today. Without His word nothing would be made. But believe upon His word. God we give you the world, as He did man in the beginning. Depend upon his word for it will guide and keep you safe. Upon His Word!

02/22/2002

Walter J. Miller

NO SECRETS

God is no secret to you. He is all seeing, all hearing, and he is all-knowing. Most of all, God is in all. Things done in darkness or behind closed doors, He knows. God knows everything. He knows you from head to toe. Why? Because He made you. God sits high and He sees everyone. There is nothing hidden from him. My brother and sisters, don't h keep secrets from the Lord. There are no secrets in His kingdom. By His blood and mercy we are saved. If you have problems carry it to Jesus. When you pray your troubles to God, He will take care of you. Believe me; it is well taken care of. Once I had
problems and troubles, I carried them to Jesus and did not look back. When you give your worries to God, Don't Worry!

02/22/2002

THE WITHER CROP

There was a man who cropped had withered for his well went dry. The river had, also, dried up. That man looked up into heaven and said, "Lord, Lord, what must I do." The Lord answered, "Pour out my Spirit over them. Speak my word over them." Then the rain came.

03/03/2002

God would provide, have a little faith

From a Sinner to a Winner

SAYINGS

The prayer of a bitter man is sweet unto thine ear, it prevails unto the heavens.

My soul abides in thee, O'Lord, hear my prayers.
O' How I love thee. All my substance comes from thee.

The world is looking for a few good men, so is the grave. Look for God and live.

Believe me when I say that the Lord is good and his mercy lasts forever. The Lord had
mercy upon me. Out of His goodness the Lord raised me up for once I was dead.

Live in the land but not of the land for your enemy will not harm you.   Sickness and
diseases will not overtake your household.

Reach high in the Lord for His height is forever. My God gave me peace and I will reach higher in that peace. I will not let the world take that away from me. I will not let friends
or people hinder me from that peace.

I am for the Lord and He is for me. We are a team.   I do not intend to have a piece of
that peace. I am going to have all of that peace. **See, feel, and touch that peace**.

2002

Let the Love of God Guide You

Walter J. Miller

STAY WITH THE LORD

How many times have you said that you were going to stick with the Lord, no matter what? Then here comes Mr. Temptation. Have no fear him. Jesus himself was tempted. There are going to be many trials and tribulation in our lives. That's why it is best to stay with the Lord. He will protect and guide you all the days of your life, as long as you stay with the Lord. I have been down many dark roads. If not for the Lord showing me His light, I would have been forever lost. Thanks be to God for his son, Jesus. I owed the world and Jesus came and gave his life for my debt. Now that I owe only Jesus because He set me free, I'm going to stay with him. The Lord will show me the way. When I am tempted the Lord would be there for me.

03/04/2002

DELIVERANCE

I left the camp of the Israelites and stayed at the camp of the Canaanites. The Lord brought me out and back to Jerusalem. I had gone through many trials and tribulations. When He brought me back, it was like a dream. Oh! How I laughed and how I sang. The Lord has done many good things for me. I was very happy. The Lord helped me to prosper again. Just like rain upon a dry land. I looked up to heaven and said," Lord you are my protector". Lord you are Jerusalem and my God for I have escaped the hunter's net. I am free through the grace of Jesus. As I cross those rivers, I thank my God for not letting me drown. I praise you and I worship you, O'Lord, in the name of your son, Jesus. He paid my debt.Thank you Jesus. In your name I am saved. When I was in trouble you were always there for me. I was in darkness and Jesus came along as the light and led me to safety for I was lost. Thank you for deliverance!

03/24/2002

FEAR NOT

Fear not my brother, when you see me walking in the neighborhood. Don't be in awe. I am not looking for dope; I am walking and praying in the community for hope. I used to be you but with prayer and God, there is hope. You can be me, fear not. I can do all things through my God who strengthen me.

03/30/2002

Walter J. Miller

MIND BEATING

Many of time since God has changed my life, I sit around and beat my mind. I will beat my mind over things such as; what did the world have to offer me? I thought I had it all.
I had all the women, drugs and money. This was my god back then. This god was supplying all my needs. At least, that is what I thought. My life now has a new meaning. I thank God and Jesus Christ for helping me turn my life around. Amen and Amen. That life I was leading was nothing compared to this life Jesus has for me now. I am happy all the time and I am very content with my life. I keep beating my mind. Why did it take me so long to know the difference between my God and their god? I don't have to beat my mind anymore. God has given me a peace of mind. This peace the world did not give to me, Jesus only. The love of God is the reason I don't have to mind beat anymore. All I have to do is keep my mind on Jesus. He died for me. Sometimes you have to beat yourself in the head and ask yourself; Why would anyone die for me or pay my debt that I owed? Now, that's mind beating!

04/14/2002

A SEEDER PRAYER

O'Lord, help me to plant the seed of life which is your Word. Help me, O'Lord, to plant the seed of truth and faith. O'Lord, all I ask is that you be my well for I know that you are the life giving water. O'Lord, send your rain and that almighty sun to reap the good harvest. O'Lord, I thank you for not letting my seed fall on stony grounds. Amen.

04/21/2002

CAST NOT THY STONE

Cast not thy stone at your fellowman. Cast not thy stone in the wind for it might return. Be careful of the stone you throw for you might hurt yourself.

My Father was King and He died and made me king.
He was King of kings and Lord of lords.

04/21/2002

Walter J. Miller

CITY LIGHTS AND COUNTRY ROADS

I was traveling the other night and notice the glamour of the city lights. The neon sighs glaring all over the place. I was in awe! Then, I went down a country road and behold there were no lights. I felt insecure. However, I felt relieved when I saw the bright lights and the glamour. Many of times I have travel down dark roads in my life, wishing for a light. They were worse than those country roads. I was in pure darkness for those roads were sinful. Many of times I cried for those city lights. Those lights guided my ways. I hope that you can understand where I am coming from. I know that here is a revelation in those city lights and those country roads. When you are living in darkness, you need to be guided by a special light. That light is not the neon or city light but it's the light that shone before Paul on his way to Damascus. Help me my brother; you know what I am talking about; leaving the good to do the bad. Help me my sister; show me that light to guide me down that country road, back to those city lights.

04/27/2002

THE FOOTSTEPS OF THE POOR

The footsteps of the poor are steps of a depressed people. Their steps are covered and guided by the Lord. They are protected through the blood of Jesus. I am poor, yet, I am rich in the Spirit of the Lord. In Him, I am never poor. The poor has no worries for their worries were nailed upon the cross. The footsteps of the poor are designated by God for He has richly blessed them. The love He has for them is strong and everlasting. Through the grace of God, the poor would never go hungry or be without. It's better to be poor and know the Lord than to be rich and don't know the Lord. I am very content with the substance from the Lord for He knows my every need. My brothers and sisters let God guide your ways for He make them both; rich and poor steps. God is the Lord of the poor; however, He loves the rich too. He made them all.

04/28/2002

Walter J. Miller

I REMEMBER WHEN

When I was a child, I remember when you could count on the season; winter, summer, fall and spring. Winter always came in time for Christmas. This was the time to bring out all overcoats and file-up the fireplace. This time was very cozy. Summertime was a time out for school, for vacation, going to see grandma and grandpa and especially going to the beach. Then we had to watch out for the storms. Now, fall was a time I did not like because night came to soon. Playtime was short. Springtime, well, all of the pretty came out to see you. All the rain started in the fall and continued into the spring. Easter was at the end of winter. When night came, it was black dark. We did not have all those streetlights. The stars were a sight to look at. I remember when I could depend on the rain in due season, the cold in the winter and the hot sun in the summer. Now, you can't tell day from night with all the lights. You can't count the stars anymore and the rain doesn't come like it used to. The seasons are out of order. There was a man who predicted this, 2000 years ago. I am very thankful for Him, for He told me many things. He told me not to be amaze for His word is true. His word will not return void. He also told me many wonders will come upon this earth before He returned. I am not surprised because I believe on His word. His word has led my life.

05/13/2002

WAKE UP TO THE SPIRIT

If you have not heard of the light, the world has you deaf. Wake up to the Spirit. If you have not seen the light, the world has you blind. If you have not felt the power of the light, the world has you dead unto the Spirit. Wake up to the Spirit. Not tomorrow, but now. There are many kinds of spirits in the world. Some spirits that has no evil in them are; the Spirit of Love, Kindness, Self-Control, and Joy. Be spiritual in your walk, my Brothers and Sisters. Let us not love after the flesh. There is no law against Long-suffering. Let your Meekness and Temperance show you the way. If you keep the Faith and have Goodness, you will have Peace all the days of your life.

05/23/2002

Walter J. Miller

MRS. HURSTON

I was inspired by the life of Ms. Zora Neale Hurston, she was a highway writer. Ms. Houston travel to and fro doing her thing, which was writing. She wrote about things that were happening in her life. Zora left her dust track in the road. I have call Moses, "Man of the Mountain", to help me follow her footsteps as a writer. Many good writers of color are not recognized until their eyes are watching God.

I admire the life of Ms. Houston. I live four blocks from her home. As a child going to Lincoln Park Academy, I believe it was called in those days Benton's Quarters, I did not know that I was passing a historic site. I love to read Ms. Houston's books for the "gramma". That was proper talking back then until some of us got a little uppity, like the white folks had taught us. To me, Ms. Houston was a legend for she left behind a legacy. Her poetry state was very rich.

I am in poetry. As a beginning writer, I hope to achieve my goal to be rich and famous. I don't want to die in despair and no one knows me. I want to keep Ms. Houston legacy alive for in Fort Pierce she was a historian among us. Ms. Zora Neale Houston, the citizens of St. Lucie County would be proud of her, if they knew her well. She is my hero.

As a struggling writer, all my work is known by the one whom inspired me to write those poems and letters. I wonder who inspired Ms. Houston because my God was in all of my writing. If not for Him, I could not write a word. I thank Him every day for his inspired word. Yes! I want the Lord to lead my writing and my life forever. Ms. Houston was very religious. I read some of her work when she spoke highly of her God. Although her life was harsh, she still had love for her God.

05/13/2002

In memories of Ms. Zora Neale Houston, she lives. May my God read all of her books and said well done.

THE HOUSE WITH HOLES

The house with holes is a house of illness, a sinful house. It takes many hands to build a house. The soundness of this house all depend on the builder. Even though it takes many hands to build a house, it only takes one hand to destroy it. The builder of truth is the only one that can build a solid house, if God has his hand in it. A house that doesn't have the love of God will not stand. It will fall. The house with holes is a house of corruption, looking for God's destruction. The house that is constructed by God will stand forever. Even if it falls, God will surely pick it up.

05/26/2002

Let God build you up. If not God, then you are damned.

Walter J. Miller

COURAGEOUS

With the world so full of corruption, it takes a lot of courage to stand against the world. There are times when the devil is trying all he can to betray you. Be strong in the Lord for He will see you through. Depend upon the one that is not corrupted. He will keep you strong in times of weakness. First you have to believe on Him. There will be days of trials and tribulation, be courageous for the Lord is with you. Seek wisdom, knowledge and understanding from the Lord. Learn to love the Lord with all your heart and soul. Take courage and follow Jesus. Let the love of God guide your life. He sent His only Son as a living sacrifice upon the cross so that you may have life. Water, blood and the Spirit has set you free, in the name of Jesus.

05/27/2002

Be of good courage.

UNTO MY BROTHERS

Unto my God I do pray. I pray for my brothers and all who don't know my Father. Unto my brothers, pray for thy sisters. They travail, also, in the Lord daily. From a brother to a brother, pray for me and I will pray for you. Keep praising God; it is good unto thy soul. Unto my brothers, teach thy brothers the ways of thy Father which art in Heaven. Unto my brothers, ask your Father for wisdom, knowledge and understanding so that you can lead them to God. Teach them to seek Him first and everything will be common place. Unto my brothers, love as my Father loves. Look around you my brothers and sisters and see the love my God show you every day, in the name of Jesus. Amen.

06/10/2002

WRONG ARMOR

Many of my brothers have on the wrong armor. Some say they are the light before their brothers. Their brothers are yet being deceived. I say to my brothers, study to show yourself approved. The devil, ole Satan, Lucifer by name is the light bearer. He was created pure next to God as His server until he became bold. He wanted to be like God. He even wanted to sit upon God's throne. My brothers, be not wearer of the wrong armor. Put on the whole armor of God. He is the light of the world. God will not deceive you. Satan has a lot of my brothers putting on the wrong armor.

06/10/2002

Walter J. Miller

PLANTATION MANNER

Well, well, let's talk about this plantation. What is a plantation? It's a place that is planted. Then why were the people not allowed to leave? Were they planted in their minds? Now, let look at manner. It is the way you act socially, the etiquette of your behavior. Manners are something practiced yet manipulated. Sit on the porch and don't go anywhere! That's a command. Well, that's what plantation manners are all about. Yes ma'm, no ma'm, yes sir, no sir. Those are the real plantation manners. These are the same manners, different plantation, yet the same owners. In this time and age it's still live. Slavery has a new name, African American. Thank God, I am an American. We accept things that are not of us as names. I am trying to open the eyes of my people to see the frame work that others have given us. Wake up my brothers and sisters; we are a people that were born of Kings and Queens. Therefore, we are Prince and Princess. I thank my God for creating me in His own image and not man. I thank God for being for me and not against me. He is for those who serve in His name. God did not say have manners but have obedience unto His word. He is the manner teacher for He will teach you in the way you must act. My God has the truth for you, if only you would read. Plantation manners are man taught, as other things that are not of God. Read the Bible for it holds all truths. Let no man betray you with the word of God. We should not be surprised of nothing in these days for the Lord said these things over 2000 years ago. There would be corruption in the church in the latter days; false teachers, preachers, even false gods. Study God's word; learn the manners of God and not of plantation.

06/02/2002

CRY FOR ME

There were times that I felt invisible, a feeling that no one could touch me. O'Cry for me. I had no regards for no one. O'Cry for me. I would laugh at people down fall. I had no respect for others. O'Cry for me. O'Cry for me, for not believing in God. Now here I lay, O'Cry for me. O'God, O'Cry for me.

06/25/2002

May the God of my Father and Mother look down on me.

RUNNING FROM GOD TO THE DEVIL

I have been running from the Lord for many years, trying to please my flesh. I know my God is not flesh. My God is Spirit. Every time I would leave my God for the devil, he would laugh. That would make him happy and my God sad. I prayed that this would stop, in the name of Jesus. You can't serve two masters at the same time. God taught me to love, not to hate. I prayed and the devil left me alone. God gave me the strength to overcome the devil's powers. Now that God have me in his care, I have peace. I don't have to worry about running from God to the Devil.

07/04/2002

PEACE!!!

Walter J. Miller

I FOUND PEACE

When my life was in trouble, I had nowhere to turn. I went through many ups and downs. My trials and tribulation were never ending. Then, I met the Lord in jail. I was there for all the wrongs I had done. I have never let go of the Lord's hand. I found peace. That peace was Jesus Christ. God sent Him to me in my darkest days. This peace was the light of Jesus. I found peace in His name. I found peace in His blood. There is nothing like peace in your life. When you love and serve the Lord, there are no worries or fears. Troubles would come but peace would help you handle it. The freedom of peace is not cheap, it will cost you. I lost many of my so call friends when I found peace. God gave me a new beginning by the blood of Jesus. I am happy all the time with this peace I found in Jesus. I knew I was not worthy of this peace, however, I went before my God with a repented heart. I call unto my God for forgiveness. He gave me peace by forgiving me all my sins. God is a merciful God. I found peace.

07/04/2002

THE WEAKER VESSEL

God made man to be like himself after His image. We are to be strong. He made that vessel and another vessel. This vessel was the weaker vessel. He made woman to be man's helpmate. There comes a time when the weaker vessel has to be strong for the stronger vessel. With the help of their God, they do past the test. I wonder why some things were not meant to be understood.

07/28/2002

Be strong my brothers and sisters for one another in Christ Jesus.

THREE BROTHERS

I had a spiritual awaking a while back and God came into my life. God changed my direction from where I was going. That place was straight to Hell. I was weak and needed plenty of strong brothers in my path. I would listen to a Christian radio station. I would listen to Brother McGee, Brother Stanly and Brother Rogers. I thank my God for those brothers. They gave me encouragement. They ministered daily over the air waves, preaching their message to all souls that would listen. Those three brothers fed me all the milk a body could drink. I even listen to Brother Kennedy and Sister Phillis, they all added to my growth. All in all, I felt strong enough to cut my radio off and go it on my own. My faith came from listening to those three brothers but I stopped and I began to waver in the word. Forgetting the things I had learn from the teaching of those three brothers, I started feeling weak. The world began to take its toll on me. When I realized I needed those three brothers back in my life, I needed to return to drinking milk all over. Through all my trials and tribulation, my God stayed there for me. He and those three brothers stayed there for me.

08/02/2002

THE ANGEL BOX OF PRAYERS

I know you have prayed many times. You prayed to your God for help. Seem like your prayers fall on deaf ears. I am here to let you know that all of your prayers are in the angel box of prayers. My brothers and sisters, just hold on to your faith in Jesus. On day the angel will pull out your prayer request.

08/18/2002

CAN'T HIDE HIM

There are a lot of us who don't want to expose God to friends. When I found the Lord I tried to hide Him. Even though, He was in my heart. He got so big even in darkness He would shine in my walk, my steps, and my talk. Everywhere I went He was there, in the name of Jesus.

08/18/2002

DEFENDING JESUS NAME

Defending Jesus, we don't have to do because He is all power. I know we forget sometimes where all our strength comes from. We need to have a little faith, in the name of Jesus. We need to believe a bit more on Him. I was caught in a situation defending myself, screaming at the top of my voice. I should have been defending the name of Jesus. The name of Jesus keeps me from stealing and begging for bread. Thank you Jesus. My God supply all my needs. We have to let the world know that we serve a mighty God who own warehouses, as many as the grains of sand on the seashore. I have the key as long as I have Jesus by my side. Father in heaven, I thank you for your Son's shared blood.

08/18/2002

BLESSED

Walter J. Miller

WHAT MY GOD SHOWED ME

The word of the Lord came to me saying, "What do you see?" I said, "An almond tree". Then the Lord said, "You have seen well, my son". The Spirit of God was on me. I heard Him say, "You are ready to spread my word, therefore, I will bless thee and I will devour those who devour you." Then I heard my God speaking saying, "I will heal all of your wounds". I heard my God speaking again saying He will break the yoke from my neck. I would no longer be a slave to sin. That's what my God showed me. My God showed me He is looking for a place to rest. My God showed me that He is looking for a place to rest. My God showed me that He wanted to rest in my heart, my soul and my mind. That's what my God showed me.

08/20/2002

Let the love of God be shown to your fellowman.

God is Love.

V.E.T. Venting Eternal Thoughts

To all my comrades out there,

I watch some of you still fighting a battle that was won over two thousand years ago. I look around and see my brothers and sisters struggling within. Their outside is fading away. They are unstable and their minds are warp. They are forever fighting against themselves. They are trying to find their way in the dark. I tell you the truth, Jesus is the way. They only have to believe and have a little faith. Be victorious in Jesus. Jesus is the light; find it, for the love of God. He sent that light to the whole world.

08/20/2002

Forever Praying For You

Walter J. Miller

KEEPING FOCUS

With all of the things going on in the world today, I ask my brothers and sisters to keep focus on the word of God. Trials may come and trials may go. Keep your focus on the Lord and He will make a way for you. Sitting here in my home, it is a very, very, peaceful place. God made it that way. I have peace in my heart, as well. I thank Him. Once I was dead and the Lord raised me up. I was down and the Lord picked me up. Keeping focus is peace within and it will show outward. My focus on the Lord keeps me going. When my trouble days comes, He is there for me. I did not lose focus even though my trials and tribulation were upon me. The Lord kept His focus on me by sending His mighty angels to me. My brothers and sisters no matter what is taking place in your life; keep your focus on the Lord.

08/31/2002

RISE UP O'GOD (You are my God)

Rise up O'God and defend my cause, you are my God. My enemy is all around me. I need you O'Lord, you are my God. I believe in you for my faith lead me to believe. Rise up O'God, you are my God. Protect me from the deadly pestilence of the world. Rise up O'God, you are my God. Let not any disease come near my house. Let not my heart be trouble for you are my God. Rise up O'God, you are my God. You open doors of happiness and peace. I thank you, in Jesus name. Rise up O'God, you are my God.

09/08/2002

CONFIDENCE

The help of the Lord has kept me. It was His hands and loving mercy that kept me strong. I know without his love I am nothing. I once was an empty shell but the Lord filled me with His love. The Lord is love and that's what gives me confidence. There are times when I would lose that confidence or faith. They are both the same. I would let that ole devil tempt me. I would be in fear of his temptation. I knew I had lost my protection. I know that my God don't lie. He promised to never leave me. My God don't do match or patch jobs. He does a complete job. Through His love and mercy; He heals you from top to bottom, from the crown of your head to the sole of your feet. That's the confidence that I have in my God. I pray for your confidence in Him. A person who has no confidence needs to depend on the Lord.

10/13/2002

A person, who lives in the shadow of another, has no confidence in himself.

THE LORD'S TRAIN

The Lord's train is nothing but the love of the Lord. God is love. Climb aboard, the Lord is the conductor. Meet us at the station for this train arrival. Be not like Moses when he saw the Lord's train he hid himself. This train is never ending. Come one, come all, and get on board. The Lord's love is everlasting. Get the ticket of your life. Find Jesus and your ride is free. Get first class seats. This train stops at all cross roads in your life.

10/14/2002

Walter J. Miller

FOOTSTEPS IN THE COMMUNITY

To all of the volunteers and my brothers and sisters in the community:

First of all, I would like to thank my God for guiding my footsteps in this program. My brothers and sisters are you ready to fill the empty footsteps in your community? Footsteps in the community must be solid. Give the kids footsteps in the community to follow. For the love of God, let's come together at this crossroad, join hands and walk side by side in making these footsteps in the community.

10/26/2002

VIOLENCE

When is the violence going to stop? When we; stop the dealers from selling their wares. When we; can stop the grownups from putting guns and drugs in some mother's child hands. It's killing some mother's child's future, past and present. The fathers have to mourn for their daughters and how a mother has to cry for her son. When is the violence going to stop?

CLEAN SHEETS

Let us not amend ourselves beneath the sheets with strange bedfellows. Let us keep a clean sheet for there
might come a day of engagement.

A DIFFERENT

There is a big difference in being a non-believer than to be partaker of something that is diverse to the word of God.

12/21/2002

BESTOWED

Bestow upon me, O'Lord, your mercy. I am not worthy of your love. Bestow upon my lips your word in my mouth. Bestow upon me the love for my brothers and sisters and let us bestow the praise upon you.

01/12/2003

Walter J. Miller

A FATHER'S LOVE

A father loves being a father, in the mold of his Father above. When he is weak, he looks to his family for strength. He shelters and protects them at all cost. That's a father's love. When he knows he has been shoved, he looks no farther than above for that Father's love. That Father's love is where he gets all his strength from. Now, all tired and worn, he has a loving arm to lean on. Sometimes up and sometimes down, yet he shows that father's love without a frown. A father loves at the end of the day. He kneels and prays, giving thanks for his family. From a Father up above to a father's love.

01/18/2003

INSPIRATIONAL THOUGHTS

Many times I have not followed my mind. Inspiration is sweet. They are words from God. Inspirational thoughts come at all times, day and night. My mind has the desire to write, but I let my heart deceive me. Many times I would wake up in the middle of the night with a thought. I would be very sleepy. I tell myself I can remember that in the morning. Of course, the next day I would have forgotten everything. When the Lord speaks to me, sometimes I would obey His calling and you know the rest. Every word I have written has come from the Lord. I thank Him for every word. Every word is inspirational. I love the Lord. He has been so good to me.

02/15/2003

RESURRECTION

I was very elated to see the joy, praise and glory the people was given Zora Neale Hurston. She once was dead, yet she lives. Ms. Hurston has been resurrected. No name calling but there was another elected one raised from the dead. You know who. They gave Him no respect until He was raised from the dead. Even in his own hometown where He fed the hungry, healed the sick and raised the dead. Zora Neale Hurston was a healer and some of her books could have raised the dead. I think black history for bringing her to the light. Her writing was a gift from her God, whom she loved very much.

02/28/2003

ENDURE

Father God, here I am in your house once again. Edify me, O'God; give me wisdom, knowledge and understanding. Feed me, Lord Jesus, with your word. Show me the way unto your courts. Teach me how to love my enemy. Show me how to love my neighbors as myself. Keep me, O'Lord, from falling away. Strengthen me Father for I am weak. Help me, Father, to overcome all my short coming, in the name of Jesus. Father God, my sins are ever before you. Rid me Father of these sinful ways. Teach me how to pray, my Father. I know you are in heaven. You are my Shepherd. You lead me daily, as I walk this land down in the valley where I face death all day long. I worry not, for you are with me. Help me Father, help me!

03/02/2003

Standing in the need of prayer.

Walter J. Miller

I'M PRAYING FOR YOU

"I will never leave you." he said, "I will be there." He told us in His word that He answers every prayer. He said that He will always love us and protect us from harm. He watches over the sparrow. Are you not more than a sparrow? I am giving you to Jesus, He cares for you. Ask Him for help and everything will be alright. Pray unto Him day and night. He is the only miracle worker. Turn to Him and He will save you.

05/20/2003

SPEAK UNTO MY SPIRIT

Speak unto my spirit, O'Lord, my soul cries out to thee. I have a feeling everything is going to be alright because the light from the light house has shine its light on me. I walk through the valley, even faced with death. God was always with me. He was my guide. The Lord leadeth me to higher grounds. He brings me into His light. I stretch my hands unto thee for under your wing I am safe. Father God, give me the love that you have. Give me that everlasting love that's in Jesus name. My brothers and sisters are crying out to me, Lord. I want to give them love. The same love that you gave the world. I love to fellowship with my brothers and sisters in love, for you are love and you are in me.

05/23/2003

I GAVE CARE UNTO THE WORLD

I once was a great sinner. I had no thought of any heavenly being. I thought I loved the things of this world. I was wrong. Then I found my Savior, Jesus Christ. Many times I gave care unto the world. Satan was my world, I thought. I did not know a better world was out there. After I found the Lord, my world was just beginning. The Lord supplied all my needs and I thank Him. The Lord has been so good to me. I can do all things through Him. Through Him all things are possible. I am in the world but not of the world. Because of the love He has for me, He is my only care.

06/03/2003

SECOND CHANCE

When you praise the Lord, He will praise you. When you walk with Jesus, He will walk with you. When you look to God, He will surely see you. His love and mercy is there at all times. He believes in second chances. Come to Jesus, He will come to you, with a second chance.

08/10/2003

IN DISPUTE

O'Lord, as my highs and lows are in dispute, help me. Don't let me get to high that you can't reach me or get to low that you can't reach down and pick me up. I took a look at Paul and how his life was in dispute. Yes, Lord, you reached way down and picked him up. O'Lord, I am in dispute, help me. My weakness is ever before me. Strengthen me. Lord you are a very merciful God. Don't dispute in helping me. I am sorry for all my sins. I ask for your grace, mercy and your loving kindness to forgiving me.

08/10/2003

FAMILY TIME

Family time is a time when the family comes together and share the love for each other. Family time is a time to communicate with each other. Family time is a time to lay aside whatever you have to do and do it with your family. God laid aside all He had to do. He gave us His love to share with each other. Family time is a time of sharing and caring. I love family time. I love being close to my family. Family time gives me strength to care and love my family. Jesus has a family, too. You! The church is His family. Being a family with Jesus means you are a family with God. Let us all come and stay together as a family.

09/13/03

LITTLE THINGS

Why worry about the big things in life? Let's look at the little thing in our life and how they are, yet so big (Hello, that small); smaller than the ant. Look how God used the smallest thing to show us how wise it can be. The ant stores its food up for the winter. He used one of the dumbest animals to speak to man; (the donkey, Numbers 22:21). God don't look at your greatness. He looks at your heart. Remember these two things: No matter how low, the Lord will pick you up and if you are raised up without the Lord, He will surely reach up and bring you down. The book of Proverbs tells us many little things that God like and don't like. It cost such a little thing to love. From a sinner to a winner, I learn to love the goodness my God has bestowed upon me. I love the little things such as; peace, happiness, love and joy. These are the little things He will give you for his love.

10/20/2003

ASKING

Open my eyes, O'Lord, guide me through this land. Keep thy promise that thy will never leave me. O'Lord, I praise thy name. You said, O'Lord, if I call upon your name and keep thy commandments, thy will heal me. Clean my ears that I may hear thee, O'Lord. Have mercy on me and forgive all my transgressions. The day cometh and I want to be with thee, O'Lord. You sought a man to carry your word unto the world. Here I am. I am asking, O'Lord, chose me. Speak unto my spirit, O'Lord for my soul cries out to thee. Heal my body, O'Lord, so that my mind will be forever thankful.

10/29/2003

Walter J. Miller

TOOLS

Ground troops are soldiers waiting on God's orders. Let not the enemies redeem the land for God's soldiers protect it. I will not let the devil or his demons demand my life. My life is command by my God.

11/02/2003

Man will sometimes put his possession in the abundance of his life.

SUBMISSIVE *(Submitting and Resisting)*

Submitting to the devil and all his demons means that you are resisting God. God said resist the devil and he will flee, however, you were submissive. Know the powers that God has given you to resist anything.

11/02/2003

WORDS

I have come over too many hills to turn around. I have suffered too many years. God has changed my life for the good. I have to thank my God and Savior, Jesus Christ. I have a God that has open up the windows of heaven and poured me out a blessing. I have listened unto my God's voice. His words are forever bound in my heart. I know I have a place in His kingdom as long as I keep and do His will. His love, mercy and grace made a change in me. He forgave all of my sins. My past is behind me. I have to look forward in his name. My brothers and sisters, you pray for me and I will do the same for you. We must build a relationship with God for ourselves. He loves you just as much as He does the other. Many of times I felt left out but He was always there.

11/05/2003

TRIBULATIONS

This day I am in the flesh, the Lord is not with me. He and I have had our difference from time to time. I wonder why? I know why, but I am afraid to admit it. My God is not pleased with the sinful part of my life. I pray daily for Him to come and rescue me. I am sorry. I am wrong for being disobedient unto my God. Help me Lord Jesus, to overcome this tribulation, in Jesus name. Amen

11/09/2003

LET GOD BE GOD

Let God be God. Many times we try to speak for God when He has not spoken to us. I speak as the Holy Spirit see fit. In the beginning was his Spirit and the Spirit was with Him. Let's all heed to his Spirit for the Spirit is God. Stay in the Spirit of God; for God is good all the time. He brings light to the darkness. Let God be God. He is truth and life.

01/04/04

Walter J. Miller

KEEPING MY BROTHER

Keeping my brother, sometimes strife gets in the way. Keeping my brother means I am my brother's keeper. Keeping my brother is hard sometimes because I have to feed him, clothe him, and shelter him. Keeping my brother. There is nothing too hard for the LORD. Many times I wonder who will keep me. If Jesus is God's Son, then He is keeping me. Jesus is all of my brothers' keeper. Keeping my brother, in the shelter of the most high, He will find rest. We all reject keeping our brothers. The Lord gave a great command; have love for one another. If you have love for your brothers then you are truly your brother's keeper. Love keeps all things together, in Jesus name. He is there for him; keeping my brother when he is going through trials and storms. Let him find love in his brother.
Father God, I ask you to let me, your son, bring my brother to you.

02/29/2004

HAVE YOUR WAY

Have your way Lord in my life. My roads are rough and my mountains are high. Have your way for I can't seem to find mine. The waters are getting higher. Through all my trials and tribulation you were there. Have your way for I remain under the shelter of the most high. I found rest in Him. I have made Him my defender. I am protected by His Angels where else I go. Many may fall by my side, but no harm will fall on me. The Lord is having his way in my life. Many times I wanted to have my way but the Lord knows best. Have your way.

03/07/2004

TODAY, TOMORROW, YESTERDAY

Remember, my brothers and sisters, today where you came from. Remember where you went yesterday and know where you are headed tomorrow. But most of all, remember your God first. He is your today, tomorrow, and your yesterday. He made them all and he is in all. So, let's not forget where we came from and where we are headed. God guides them all. So praise God every day. It was yesterday you were born and today you live. Remember the next day is not promised to anyone, not today, tomorrow or yesterday. Start praising Him today. Maybe e will forgive you for what you did yesterday and start blessing you tomorrow.

THINKING OF PRESENT, PAST, FUTURE
TODAY, TOMORROW, YESTERDAY
SPIRIT, MIND, SOUL
These are things that makes up a man's body; his spirit, his mind, and his soul. A man lives for the present trying to forget his pass. Yet, he still looks to the future, thinking about today, trying to remember what yesterday was all about. Where did he go wrong?

He doesn't want to make that same mistake tomorrow. Seeking knowledge of the present, past and future; for his spirit, mind and soul, needs understanding for today, yesterday and tomorrow. He will succeed, if he has wisdom of the present, past and future of today, yesterday and tomorrow, that would keep his spirit, mind
and soul.

Walter J. Miller

THE UNINSURED DRIVER

I say, "Come ride with me for a while." The ride is short but the journey is long. I rode with you for a while as an uninsured rider driven by an uninsured driver. I say, when you are on that road and not insured by Jesus and bonded by God, you have no benefits. When you ride or pick up those uninsured passengers; Mr. Devil or Ms. Satan, your insurance doesn't cover them. So don't ride them and don't let them drive!

So, be insured by God so that you are covered by Him. Let Jesus be your passenger and let Him drive you. He is bonded by God.

So, I say, all you uninsured drivers and uninsured riders, you better get some crises insurance that is bonded by God and assured by Jesus. It covers you; it never expires or cancels, as long as you stay in touch with your
insurer… that is Jesus!

REVELATION

Knowing the revelation of God and learning how He works in your life is very essential, especially when you need guidance of your ways in life. Sometimes, you might not understand the things that happen in your walks, trials and tribulations. So, if you learn to reveal God's revelation, things would be much easier. If you don't then you would have to depend on your own revelation, which is not from God. You are then misled away from God's revelation. It's good to know about God and to get a good understanding of His revelation. You should read your Bible so no one will lead you astray and your walk will be so much better. It's all God's revelation. Learn it. Keep it in your heart and mind so your ways will not lead you into darkness and your troubled days would be few. The Bible is the true doctrine of His word and His revelation of how you should walk in life among your brother and sisters. Let them know how the revelation of God works in their lives. Keep His true doctrine alive with His revelation.

Walter J. Miller

THE MISSING PIECE

My life was a puzzle, a jigsaw one at that. The missing piece was a piece I thought I would or could find. I had no peace in my life until I found that missing piece. That piece was Jesus. After finding Him, I was one whole puzzle and I had peace in my life. That peace is my God, my Lord and my Savior. I thank Him for helping me find this peace in my life. I was corrupted. Now, I have peace with my brothers and sisters. I love them as myself. Jesus says, with this piece; loving my brothers and sisters and my neighbors, I will have peace in my heart and in my life. If you have a missing piece in your life, ask your God to help you find it. He will give you peace. That piece is Jesus. Missing pieces may be hard to find because you are not looking in the right places. Look to Jesus for that missing piece in your life. He will surely give to you a kind of peace that you will never forget. That missing piece could hurt so badly but your God has found that missing piece in your life. It will bring you to a full life of peace.

Praise Him! Thank Him for being that missing piece!

SPIRITUAL FOOD

If you are hungry for Jesus, you don't need the devil's food. It will not fill you up. If you let God feed you, you will stay full. You will never hunger or thirst again, spiritually or physically. He did it for me; He will do it for you. For once in my life, I am full and I am still eating of this spiritual food. I am being spiritually fed. He is nursing me with milk. With my faith in Him, one day I will be able and ready for solid food, to keep me growing. The food Jesus feeds me will keep me strong and give me virtue and great stature. When He sends me out to work, I will be able to withstand the fire and show

myself approved. He has put on me His whole armor, which will protect and be my defense. This armor will carry me through, as I walk with Jesus, and keep me strong. If I can't do the job or I get weak, I will ask Jesus to feed me a little more to give me strength. If I don't know, then I will ask Him for wisdom, knowledge and understanding. So, I can keep on doing His work. With His spiritual food, it will keep me spiritually and physically strong.

Walter J. Miller

STEPS

Steps are something that carry us to, from and around in this world. Some steps are murky some are shaky, some are weak and some are strong. Some disappear in broad daylight and some reappear at night. Could these steps be guided by something or someone higher than us? Yes! I think so. Your shaky and murky steps are weak. They are led by your own selfish desire. Your solid steps are strong. They are led by God. There are good steps in life and there are bad ones. Sometimes good steps are misguided because they step to the left or step to the right instead of keeping straight. Some steps are guided by God. All good steps are guided by Him; however, our adversary can guide our steps, too. So, we must determine which steps we take in our daily life, as we walk toward Jesus. Let us not walk in darkness or step off from the light. Let us keep all of our steps in the right direction by taking these steps with Jesus. He will guide your every step. He will not let you stumble. If you do, He will pick you up. You have to take that step towards Him. My brother, He is your best guide and your friend. So, walk with Him for He will not lead you wrong.

THESE ARE HELPFUL STEPS TOWARD A SPIRITUAL LIFE

1. Matthew 9:12-13   My God came to save the ones that are lost.

2. Matthew 20:29-34   My God came to give me light out of my darkness.

3. Mark 5:35-36   My God is my Resurrection.

4. Luke 1:37   I depend on my God for everything.

5. Luke 5:13   He will make me clean.

6. Luke 18:35-43   Even the blind will be able to see

7. John 3:14-18   My God sent His Son to save me.

8. John 6:28-29   He is my Bread of Life.

9. John 6:68-69   I plan to stay with my God.

10. John 7:37-39   He is the Life Giving Water.

11. John 8:12   He is my Light.

12. John 10:9-10   My good Shepherd.

13. John 11:25-26   He is my Life.

14. Acts 3:16   Faith in Jesus.

15. Acts 4:12   He is my Salvation.

16. Acts 4:16-31   I must believe in Him.

17. Romans 8:38-39   I am His sheep.

18. I Corinthians 1:18-25   His wisdom is great.

19. I Corinthians 15:20-22   He has all power.

20. II Corinthians 1:8-11   He will answer my prayers and I will give Him thanks.

21. II Corinthians 5:21   He gave His life for me.

Walter J. Miller

22. Galatians 1:4   He set me free.

23. Ephesians 2:4-5   He is a forgiving God.

24. Philippians 2:13   He is always working in me.

25. Colossians 2:13-14   He crossed out my debt.

26. Hebrews 2:14-18   He is my Protector.

27. Hebrews 7:24-25   God let his Son be that Sacrifice.

FOREVER BURNING

O'Father, the fire and love that I have for you in my heart is forever burning. I know that I love you and I know that you love me. That love is forever burning.

12 TIMES 12

Over less than a century ago, I had a choice to do my first 12-step program. This was school, but I fail. I was a student of society. I decided to let my teacher, the world, teach me. You did not have to be a scholar to be in the world class. You would never graduate or get a diploma, but you can excuse yourself from the world. I never finish the class of the world. I found myself gazing at the world for she was a thing to see. After being such a failure, I drop out for good. When I went back to school, the principal would not let me back in. He said I was too old for teaching. I tried on my own and failed myself. I tried to come up with 12 times 12 out of fifty years, I still could not. I decided to enter a new 12-step program. This time I have a new teacher and principal that will accept me back no matter how many times I fail. My principal name is Jesus and my new teacher name is Wisdom. She is great for she will teach you what 12 times 12 is. If you love her, she will give you her wisdom, knowledge and understanding of all her ways. Her doors are always open to her learning and the principal will always let you back in to start over again. My teacher's wisdom will always teach you virtues of life and how to do math. Whether I fail or finish this 12-step program, I thank my God for being that principal in my life. I thank Him for letting me know that I can always come back for life. It may take a hundred and forty four times to get it right. That is 12 times 12.

Walter J. Miller

12 STEPS

I went back over the twelve steps one by one and asked myself this question; how is my life unmanageable?

1. My life is out of control with my addiction.

2. In my search for a power greater than me, which was my God, it was my decision to let go and let it be God's will.

3. As I understand Him: First to understand someone you have to know them and trust them. Then, I ask myself, do I really know this God which is so forgiving
And so loving?

4. A God that will forgive me all my past wrong.

5. To admit to Him and someone else all my wrongs.

6. Because I was willing to let Him heal me of my addiction.

7. Yes! I asked Him to heal me.

8. I asked Him to forgive me and all the people I had hurt in my past life.

9. I went to them and asked forgiveness and was willing to make things right with them.

10. I needed to keep a daily check on myself, in my daily activities, to make sure I didn't harm myself or others.

11. I prayed to my God in my daily prayers to give me strength that I may do His will and not mine. In my healing,

I may walk closer with Him during my trials and tribulations.

12. I can help those who stand alone in their addiction, so they may learn, also, to depend on their higher power.

Some do not have a higher power. I thank God for sending me Jesus, in my fight of recovery. I have a closer walk with Jesus. He is my only power. If I turn back to my addiction, I am doomed. That's why daily I ask my God to keep me strong and keep healing me. I still have many open wounds in my life that needs healing. That's why I keep on praying. It's going to take one day and one step at a time. So, just keep praying and walking with your higher power. That higher power is the Lord Jesus.

Walter J. Miller

4 C's - DRUGS OF CHOICE

Yes! My brothers, you once guided my life with your four C's; Crack, Crank, Cash and Crime! This led me out of control to condemnation. So now, my brothers, let me guide your life with my four C's: Christ, Christ, Christ and Christ. Your C's changed, but this one will never change. I was led down a dark road by your Crack, Crank, Cash, and Crime. How terrible it was for me. It led my life to the brink of death; spiritually and physically. I knew that there was no point of return. I found myself out of control and in pure darkness. I don't need your Crack, Crank, Cash and Crime anymore! I stopped and let go. Then I started all over again with my Christ. He kept me high. He led me to the light. He kept money in my pockets and no worries. With this Christ, I learn to love myself and others. With Crack, Crank, Cash, and Crime, I didn't love either. Now, I am Concerned, Cool, Calm and Collected. So now, my brother, come get high with me and my best friend, Christ, Christ, Christ and Christ. It's your past, present and future. This is a lifetime invitation!

A SINNER'S PRAYER

O'Lord, you said where I go you will go with me and wherever I put my hands or feet you would guide me. O'Lord, you said, if I call upon the name of Jesus for anything you would answer my prayer. O'Lord, I look to you for all my help. Glory to you, O'Lord. You are my best friend. I thank you, in the name of Jesus. Your Son made it possible for me by dying on the cross. O'Lord, you are mine and mine alone. O'Lord, touch my heart and mind. O'Lord, heal me that I may overcome this sin. O'Lord, in the name of Jesus, I am sorry for offending you after you have been so good to me. Please forgive me of this sin. I love your ways. Forgive me for I am that I am a sinner. O'Lord, hear my prayer.

Walter J. Miller

O'STUDENT OF MINE

O', come now O'Student of mine,
Let me teach you the doctrine of the true divine. For if you have an ear to listen, O'Student of mine,
Learn of wisdom, knowledge, and understanding.
And bind them in your heart, O'Student of mine.

For wisdom will guide and knowledge will keep you, And understanding will help you, O'Student of mine.
For once I was a child in my Father's house, And he taught me the doctrine of the true divine.
O'Student of mine.

For I had an ear and I listened.
I learned wisdom, knowledge and understanding And today they guide me, protect me, and defend me.
O'Student of mine.

For I carried them in my heart, O'Student of mine.
Let not your heart be troubled.
Trust in the doctrine of the true divine, it is not my will,
But thine, O'Student of mine.

If you have ears, then let them hear The true doctrine of the true divine, That was taught to kings to lead his people.
O'Student of mine.

Learn of a truth that will guide and protect you at all times,

O'Student of mine.

INSTILL

Instill God's care in your life. Pursuit Him at all cost for He is your best friend. He is wisdom, knowledge and understanding, Seek it at all cost. Instill his love for your fellowman. From a Friend to a Friend, in the name of Jesus.

I AM A TREE

I grew tall and wide till I reached the sky.
Would you like to come and sit under me? I will shade thee.
O' come swing with me, I will make you happy.

The rain and sun came and nourished me.
I became stronger than can be, my roots spread.
Deep from B.C. to A.D., I am a tree.

Even the angels praised and adored me. Even the prophets, the righteous and unrighteous,
Leaned on me.

Yes, they even used my leaves to heal,
For I am a tree.

Look at my limbs and branches. Are they not beautiful?
These scribes wrote of me, Kings and Queens knew of me.
They all depend on me.

I was there at the beginning of time,
Even birds built houses in. Other animals nest beneath me; Some rooted in my roots.

Walter J. Miller

At fed many with my leaves and roots,
I am a tree.
Would there be a stamp of me?
Or would there be a tree greater after me?

I have given my word to all.
I wonder how I can be and who planted me.

Could it have been the Almighty?

WISE SAYINGS

1. Go not into the house of the wicked.
2. Don't drink water from the wicked, for their water can be sweet, yet bitter.
3. When thy are lost; asked not thy neighbor.
4. When thy need a friend, seek the Lord.
5. Get wisdom, along with understanding then you will have knowledge.
6. Listen to thy father and mother for your burden would be few.
7. Be not dismayed by people of the world today.
8. Humbled thyself and deliver yourself to Jesus.
9. Walk not in the ways of this world.
10. Let not thy tongue be your downfall.
11. Speak truth of thy friends and neighbors and they won't curse you.
12. Ransom not thyself, but into the Lord.
13. Be not thy own guide, let God do it.
14. Be not more than your maker.
15. With open ears, your Father hears you.
16. With open arms, He will receive you.

O' Father, God I thank you for everything in my life good and bad alike.

Walter J. Miller

TURN IT AROUND

Turn all those negatives around. Take those tests, turned them into testimonies. Take that mess, turn it into a message. That life away from God, turn it around to God. Asked Him to help you to accept the things that you can't change. Pray to your God for strength to help you turn it around. He loves you. You must believe and trust in Him, for He is an on time God. Don't depend on the world to turn it around, leave it to Him. Be unto Him what you want Him to be to you, a friend.

My brothers and sisters let God turn your life around.

THE CHILDREN

For the children's sake, let's love each other. That's what God said. Love the children. When you love them, you love Me! You hurt them, you hurt Me. I Am That I Am love! For if you have a love, as big as a mustard seed; you have big love for children and great love for a people. God don't like dirty love for the children.

PSALMS AND PROVERBS

1. Psalms 18:16-19... My Protector
2. Psalms 7:8... I Trust in Him.
3. Psalms 27:11-14... He Is My Shelter
4. Psalms 46:1-3... He Covers Me in the Storm
5. Psalms 71:1-3... He Is My Refuge
6. Psalms 107:27-31... He Is a Caring God
7. Psalms 107:41-43... He Is a Living God
8. Psalms 109:21-27... He Is My Defender
9. Psalms119:123-125... I Am His Service
10. Psalms 119:162-166...I Will Keep Your Law
11. Psalms 119:121-130...He Is My Protector and My Best Friend
12. Psalms 139:1-16...He Is All Knowing and Caring
13. Psalms 149:4...I Will Praise His Name
14. Proverbs 2:2-15... He Gives Wisdom, Knowledge and Understanding
15. Proverbs 1:7...Because I Have Knowledge of Him
16. Proverbs 2:13-16...Stupid People Have No Knowledge
17. Psalms 30:10-12...Thanking My God for What He Has Done for Me
18. Psalms 31:9-10...Turn All My Care over to God
19. Psalms 31:22...Having Faith in My God
20. Psalms 34:18...My Courage in My God
21. Psalms 38:1-9...I Must Be Still with My God
22. Psalms 39:4-5...I Must Learn to Trust My God
23. Psalms 40:17...I Must Pray
24. Psalms 42:6-8... He Is My Defender
25. Psalms 44:15-16...My Protector for a Reason
26. Psalms 55:48... God Protects Me
27. Psalms 69:1-4...Turn to Jesus

Walter J. Miller

IN THE NAME OF JESUS

Trust in the Lord for He is your best friend. Hold onto His mighty hands and don't let go. The world is waiting on you to keep you away from your God. Be free from this world. Jesus is the truth and the truth has set you free.   AMEN.

O'LORD HELP ME

O'Lord, here I am in my father's house and I have diversion in my heart. O'Lord, take this demonic spirit away from me. I want to serve you with one mind. O'Lord, I am shut up within. Please deliver me from this pit of hell. I will praise your name for the mercy of your love. O'Lord help me!

FROM BEHIND THE WALL

I thought I had security from behind that wall. One day I founded out, that wall was not built on a solid foundation. It was not concrete. One day that wall came tumbling down. I had no security! I was afraid from behind that wall. I was insecure. I had nothing to hide behind until I had a spiritual awakening. I found a wall that could not be broken down. That wall was my God, Lord and Savior; Jesus Christ. This wall was not visible but it was around me day and night. This wall was solid.
It had plenty of concrete. I have security behind this wall.

GOD IS OUR REFUGE AND STRENGTH IN TIME OF TROUBLE

Trust in the Lord. Lean not on your understanding. In all your ways acknowledge Him for the Lord is your shield. He is planted like a tree by the river. God is your refuge and strength in a time of trouble. The Lord is good and merciful. Amen.

THE FIERY FLAME

Yes! I have heard of the fiery flame. The one Moses spoke about. I did not know it was the purity of God's name; **I AM THAT I AM** the fiery flame that purifies you. Yes, I am the fiery flame that will destroy you. I am that burning desire that's in mankind. In me is that flame. I will sacrifice unto my God, myself. I will allow that fiery flame to purify and guide me. I am that, I am a being of the fiery flame. It is purity of God's name…the fiery flame.

STRENGTH PRAYER

Which of me belongs to God?
For what God has cleansed, let no man take away.
For no weapon shall prosper against me; For I have the ability of Jesus within me.
For I am an overcomer of the world, in Jesus name.

Walter J. Miller

THE VOID

Yes! Jesus filled the void in my life, through writing when I was going through my trials and tribulations. Yes! I have written many letters, all inspired by God. It really filled in for loneliness, idle time, and a lot more. He's been my inspiration. Being His scribe is a full time job. Writing for Him has filled that void in my life and keeps me happy. Jesus has been so good to me in every way. I can't go on without His help. I don't know how I could or would have filled that void without the help of Jesus. Let God fill that void in your life. I hope and pray that you would let Him be that empty part of your life. I love you all, in the name of Jesus. Filling the Void.

THE RUNNER

I thank my God! I don't have to look back anymore as I run this race. I was in a race where I thought I was the best runner but always behind. Now, I am in a race where I know I am the worst runner; however, with the help of my God, I am ahead. I don't have to worry about looking back. Peter looked back when he was walking the water to meet Jesus; however, Jesus reached out and picked him up. Yes, I was walking too and stumbled. He reached out with loving hands and I thank Him. Now, I must keep my eyes set straight on Jesus. I am running for Him, again. I know He is waiting for me at the finish line with my victory prize. Lord give me strength to run this race with my eyes wide open. I see my God is waiting there for me. I learn the true value of running a good race. You have to be patient. You can't turn left or right or even stumble. Thank God, His love and mercy will see me through. I am running this race trying to reach that finish line so I can get that trophy. The crown of glory. I must obey all the rules, if I want the prize; the crown of glory from my God.

FAITH

To have faith, you must believe in the unseen. I pray for this faith daily from my God. I ask for faith and determination so I can keep my eyes set straight on Jesus. So, I won't let myself be discouraged in my struggle with the devil and the powers of this world. I will suffer from human many times over; however, my God will make it joyful unto me. I have run my race of faith, in Jesus name. To get faith; first you must ask your God for wisdom, knowledge and understanding. I know my race of faith has been won and my Father is pleased with his child. I thank my God for giving me that faith and determination in running this race of faith and keeping my eyes set on Jesus.

Keep the faith! Run that race, as if, there were no tomorrow.

Walter J. Miller

MAMA'S WORDS (To Mama)

I remember longtime ago, when I was a sinful person with an addictive habit and sinful ways. I went to Mama for help. I don't remember her telling me nothing about her God. She did tell me nobody was going to help me unless I stop sinning and using drugs. She did not say anything about a higher power. She had been through the same thing I was going through, at that time. Only on a different level. As a child I can remember part of her live very well. Now that her higher power has changed her, she was living a better life. Praise God for that. She had become a good Christian. I guess she did not want to direct me to her higher power. Why? She would say, "If you stop doing those sinful things somebody would help you. I always thought that blood was thicker than water. I was wrong. I rather have water any day. Yes! That life-giving water, then I would thirst no more. That blood was already gone before me for all my sins. I wish Mama would have told me so. I would never forget Mama's words. My God had already shed his blood for us so that we could have life more abundantly. We will be able to drink from the everlasting cup. Mama would never explain the meaning of, "Nobody is going to help you unless you stop being sinful and using drugs. Those were Mama's words. Thanks go to my God for listening to my cry and prayers. I thank Him for helping me out of my sins of addition. As I write this letter, I am crying because I can still hear Mama's words. Well Mama, my God did help me. I love you Mama. May God bless you. Now that you are gone back to your Higher Power, I wish you were here to see me now. You can see the same God that lifted you up, did the same for me. I am trying to live right Mama. I'm hoping to meet you in heaven, so we can talk. These were Mama's words.

TAIL NO MORE

I once was at the tail end of everything in my life. I always was behind on what was happening all around me. I would catch the tail end of everything. I was the last one to find out that I was serving the wrong god. I started studying, and then I had a spiritual healing. My God opened my eyes. Now, I am not the tail no more. By studying and showing myself approve, I am the head, with Jesus as my Pilot. Thanks to the name of my God, Lord and Savior. Once I was the tail, but thanks to Jesus, I am the tail no more. I am the head and not the tail. I thank my God for turning my life around, in the name of Jesus. He came and died so we will be the tail no more. Through His Almighty Power, we are the tail no more.

Deuteronomy 28:13

CHANGING TIDE

I remember in the book of Job and in the book of Joshua, there were two Saints caught up in the changing tide. God lifted them up. I, also, remember that their adversary was in between that changing tide to devour whoever. God asked him, "Where do thy cometh." and he replied," To and fro." So, don't get caught in that changing tide. There is a changing tide in everyone's life. Satan is going to be caught up in that changing tide, by God Almighty, in that tide of fire. He got caught up in that changing tide when he stated, "I will be like the most high". I will ascend into the heavens and sit upon the throne of the Almighty. There are a lot of good and bad and those changing tides. They change because they were willing to change by the God Almighty. He alone knows why they change. God is in those changing tides, and it willed through him that they change. They come and go, bring in and taking away the good and the bad. Sometimes, a changing tide can be for the good and sometimes for the bad. With the grace of God, it was for my good. It washed away all my wrongs and cleanses me. That changing tide changed my life. Let that changing tide change for the good in your life. Don't be caught in that changing tide.

So finally, my brothers and sisters, be strong and put on the whole armor of God for we fight against dark powers of this world

WALTER'S GOD

Do you not know Walter that it was your God who created the stars you see? He knows how many there are, Walter. He called them by name just like He called you by name. Do you know or haven't you heard that your God is the everlasting God? He created the whole world and everything in it. He loves you so much, Walter. He gave his only begotten Son that you may live. He never grew tired or weary. No one understands His love for you, Walter. Who was it that made all this happen? Walter's God! He was there in the beginning and will be there in the end. Walter, my server, you are my child. I have chosen you. I brought you from your sin of addition. I've call you from the furthest corner of the earth and said to you, "Walter, I am that I am your God and you are my servant. I did not reject you, but chose you. So, do not be afraid. I am with you. I am your God, Walter. Let nothing terrified you. I will make you strong and help you. I will protect you. Those who are angry with you will know shame and defeat. Walter, those who fight against you will be defeated. They would know that I am Walters God.

STRANGERS NO MORE

I once was a stranger to my God and a friend to the world. It was one of the biggest mistakes of my life. The world did not love me. They just used me and kept me away from my God. My God came and rescued me from the world. When I followed the world, I did as the world did. I was in total darkness. There was no light in my life for a while. One day, I had a spiritual awakening and my prayers were answered. We made a promise to each other and the rainbow seal that promise between me and my best friend. I know that the storm is over for we are strangers no more. I am thankful that we are the best of friends. We have a very personal relationship. I am free of the world. What a friend I have in Jesus. I thank my God that we are strangers no more.

P.S. In the name of Jesus, my brothers and sisters; be not a stranger to your God. He is your best friend. Search your heart, your mind and seek His face. It is still the same today, as it was yesterday and will be the same tomorrow.

Walter J. Miller

LUKEWARM

Many people call themselves Christians and say they have religion. They do not understand the Word of God. They are being deceived by the churches. The church is leading you down a path of darkness. They are caught up in their own selfish desire. That's why they are not hot or cold for they are lukewarm. They have these sophisticated educated teachers who don't understand the Word of God. They are program to deceive God's people. They went to school to get a certificate to show you they have authority to deceive you. It is all being taught by man and not God. They are not hot for God's Word nor are they warm to hear what the Spirit is saying to the churches. If you have an ear, listen to what God is saying to the churches about being lukewarm. So, be hot for your God's Word. Be not lukewarm. Maybe your God will look down upon you when it's time for forgiveness. Do not straddle the fence. Don't let your cross roads keep you away from your God. Know whether to turn right or left. Be hot for Jesus and cold for the devil. You can't be lukewarm. This means you are trying to serve two masters. You either love one and hate the other. Now, that's being lukewarm.

I AM YOURS

Here I am O'Lord, Take me, and make me what you want me to be. I am yours; I am that I am your sheep. You are my Shepherd. I want you to be my Master and
me your servant. I Am Yours.

TO DRINK FROM THAT CUP

Life is sweet, even kind, it can be bitter. Life has so many different bends, it all depends. Are you ready to drink from that cup? People have good luck. They have bad luck, too. It all comes from that same cup. It all comes from the same God. People come and people go, yet, they refused to drink from that cup. You have to be strong. You have to be blessed by God and have the Spirit of Jesus within yourself to drink from that cup. Our trials and tribulations come from that cup. Jesus drank from that cup. Are you better than He? Life and death, light and darkness comes from that same cup. Are you ready to drink from that cup?

Walter J. Miller

BIBLE PROPHECIES

1...Worldwide Television Communication-Revelation 119:10

2...Israel Surrounded by Enemy Arab Nations-Psalms 83:4-8

3...Worldwide Famine-Revelation 6:5-6; Matt. 24:7

4...Daily Pestilence Kill One Fourth of the Earth-Revelation 6:8; Matt 24:7

5...Increase in Earthquakes in Strange Places-Revelation 6:12-15

6...Increase in False Messiah-Matthew 24:4-5

7...Explosion of Prophets and Heresies-Matthews 24:22

8...Rise of Anti-Semitism Worldwide-Matthew 24:9-10

9...Men's Hearts Failing Them for Fear-Luke 21:20

10...Asia Developing 200 Million Men's Army-Revelation 9:14-16

11...Euphrates River Dried Up-Revelation 16:12-14

12...A Military Highway Across Asia-Revelation 9:14-15; 16:12-14

13...Society Accepts Perversion Civics As Normal   II-Timothy 3:1-3;Rev 9:20-21

14...Ecological Devastation of the Planet-Revelations 11:18

FOR THE BLOOD OF JESUS

For the blood of Jesus is against you! Proclaim this message to the people. They have not obeyed the word of God. By not keeping His commandments, which is a grave offense, it's a strike against your life and your soul. The blood of Jesus is against you. Did you not know that every time you commit a sin you re-crucify Jesus all over again? Why nail God back to that cross. That's what you are doing every time you sin. Would you want to be part of the world that crucified your God and mine? Would you want to be the one to pierce Him in his side? Cast lots for his garment or put the crown of thorns upon is head. Would you be like Pilate and wash your hands and have nothing to do with Jesus? He was the biggest scapegoat of all time. He took the sins of the world upon Himself. That is why the blood of Jesus is against you.

MALE AND FEMALE FALSE PROPHETS

God spoke to Ezekiel and said, "Look among your men and women, denounce them and tell them to listen to what the Spirit is saying to the church." The foolish prophets are doomed. They make up their own prophecies for a few dollars more. They deceived God's people with their chanting, beads and scarves. They provide their own inspiration and they invent their own vision. They tell lies to God people. Their visions are false and so are their predictions. They claim to speak God's message but He has not spoken to them. They want to control people lives when they desire, but the blood of Jesus is against them. They hurt those who don't deserve to be hurt. God said he will rip away their control over his people and set them free. They prevent evil people from given up their evil ways. *I am against them for deceiving my people. The weapon you have form against my people will not prosper. I am coming to rescue my people. So, your false vision and predictions are over. You know that I AM THAT I AM, the Lord, God of my people. The blood of Jesus is against you male and female false prophets. I am your Lord and Savior. It is by my blood that you live and have life more abundantly.* By His grace and mercy you live. Don't be a male or female profit.

Keeping watch and holding on to his faith.

THE DREADFUL ROAD

This road, you can ride or walk down. It holds a lot of memories, to my imprisonment and to my freedom. Yes! It was a cruel and cold road. Too many, it was pain. To some it was joy. To some never to return. Talking about trials and tribulations, this road was it! Hard and cold, some love this road. Even though it was hard, some could, and some could not handle this road. Many times I had to face this road. With no respect of love for this road, it was a living hell. Some were violent. Some died at the dreadful road. It used to love and welcome me back; however, it was different this time. I met this friend, not new and not old. He always was there at this dreadful road. We became the best of friends. We did everything together. He taught me a lot. He taught me how to handle this dreadful road. This road was nothing compared to the road He was preparing me for. This road was my training ground. This friend was the best friend I ever had or found at this dreadful road. I remember that I left Him behind many times before. I asked myself, "Does He stay there at that dreadful road", because He is always there for anyone who needs Him. He loves personal visits, no mail and no calls. I wish I could take Him with me this time so that I would not have to come back down this dreadful road, again to fine Him. Maybe this time I will make Him a new home in my heart. Then I know He would be there for me. We'll be there for each other. With his help, He would lead me down a peaceful road. I won't have to return to this dreadful role.

Walter J. Miller

THE SILENT WARFARE

Look around you and see the silent warfare going on among you today. There is no big boom you hear or no push of a button. It's www.silentwarfare.com. Today's technology is very impressive. With the computers and data collected on each individual, the damage is being done silently. It's the mental and physical manipulation that's going on, the emotion part of it. How silently they are controlling the world with the war they are ragging against mankind. The government, your so call friend, is gearing up to destroy everyone that is weak and uneducated. He is teaching those of the elite a fool proof education to use against those less educated. With this silent war only the strong will survive. My brothers and sisters, the Bible lays it all on the line when it said to study and show yourself approve. Listen, Saints of the most high God, don't let this happen to the lost sheep of JEHOVAH ROHI for He is my Shepherd. Church it's time for you to take a stand against such silent warfare. The teaching of God's word starts at home. Saints there's a warfare going on out there one that can't be heard in the streets. There is a huge amount of casualties, walking dead in front of you. In the name of Jesus, open your eyes look around you to see what's happening in the world today. We act as though the Bible says everything is okay, when it's not. People are being betrayed by what they are hearing not by what they are seeing. They are not listening to the words of the Almighty, JEHOVAH JIREH, for His conviction shall come to pass. His prediction must come true. So, let Jehovah guide your life. He alone can stand up for you in this world, in this silent warfare. It is taking a toll on the people unaware. Have faith in His word for He will bring all those evils to past. This warfare will be defeated by the Almighty God. With all this war of electronic and computers, the whole world economy is at stake. Let them kill the energy of the world but don't let them kill the energy of God. Therefore, let's all pray unto thy God. The Great Jehovah.

Walter J. Miller

WITHIN A NAME

Within a name such as: Mr. President, First Lady, The Supreme Judge, or what about the Almighty or The Champion? It's all within a name. There is powerful within a name. There is prestige within a name. There are basics to be upheld within a name. Mr. Miller or Mrs. Miller is a title that you adorn with glee. There is a lot of judgmental of your character within a name. Because all eyes are on you, you will have to walk according to what's within a name. Respect and honor like the name of Jesus. Names are given in respect of what you represent. Sometimes you might fall short of the holding within a name. You have to be careful of the name you represent. God, Man, Woman or whatever, it's all within a name.

TIMES OF FAITH

When times and things are rough and everything seems hard to bare, you are not alone. There are a lot of righteous and unrighteous people out there going through the same thing. Why? Maybe there is a reason and a season for everything to happen. Maybe it is a wakeup call or a time to build up or a time to tear down. It could be time for you to get in touch with your God. You are caught out there in the middle of the storms with no protection and no umbrella. In this life, to be safe from the storms of life, you must stay under the umbrella for protection. That umbrella of protection is the Lord and Savior, Jesus Christ. So, be not dismayed, when times of faith fall short and the storms come. Turn to your God for protection and ask Him in faith to shelter you from these storms of life. He will, if only you have a little faith. Prayer alone won't help. You have to have both. To start a fire with wood you need fire. Faith and prayer can be a companion in your life. When you don't have anybody else, they go together. Like fire and wood, they are a team. So, keep up your faith in God and pray to Him. He is your best friend. Surely, He will hear you. He loves you. He wants you to show that love with faith.

FELLOWSHIP

My Father says to greet your brother with a friendly kiss, if he bears no burden. If he bare burdens embrace him and bare his pain. Then, it will be no more. Then you have shown brotherly love toward your brother. You showed him love, which your Father gave you. So, let not your brother suffer. If he falls pick him up. If he have not, give. If he know not, teach him. If he is lost, find him. Teach him love, faith and hope. Teach him to depend on the three in life: the Father, love; the Son, strength; and the Holy Spirit, power. These three are valuable to you. In your inspirational life, keep them around your neck. Your Father will be proud of you. I AM THAT I AM is coming back to see how much fellowship you have kept among your brothers. Did you lose strength? Yes! Fellowship with one another and share each other's burden. Teach each other about true doctrine. My brother, search these things out for yourself. Show yourself approved. Be under the obligation of no man. Let no man lead you astray. God is your only obligation. He is your best friend. So, let's fellowship with Him. He will take care of you and give you strength for life.

Walter J. Miller

MY ANONYMOUS JOURNEY

As I walk through the pages of life, I asked my God to help me to turn over a new leaf. A leaf of recovery. In a walk with Jesus, the recovery includes building a new me. I am powerless over my sin of addiction. I made a decision to give my life to God, so that He can build a solid foundation for my spiritual home. I was spiritually sick. I made an inventory of myself, to bring that hurt, sickness and pain to my God, I AM THAT I AM, for healing. My God came especially to save me from my sin. I call Him my Savior. I admitted to my God all my sins. I became ready for His healing. I recognize my healing. The most important time is one day at a time. That day is for the Lord's lost sheep which He has found. So, let's be happy and celebrate for a new creation is born. Let us pray to God. I have learned the essentials of prayer to God. I began to see God as a true friend. I learn the importance of the Bible as my spiritual food; the importance of sharing with others, and how to find new friends and strength. I began to appreciate and understand my body discipline because my undisciplined body drove me to insanity. I learn to fast effectively, controlling the appetite of my body with God's help. I chose my over-coming with my God; to maintain the maintenance of my daily life and to lean self-control by taking a personal inventory of myself. Through the power of my God, I will keep an eye on my future areas that I know I'm weak in. I learn to take everything to my God. With His help I learn to realize that prayer and meditation keeps me close to Him. I learn the true meaning of love. I'm not the only one in this struggle. I've experienced the true healing of God and his Holy Spirit. So let your journey begin with God.

NO ONE BUT YOU, O'LORD

O'Lord, here I am again in worse shape than ever before. I am at my cross road and my life is so torn. I left you. O'Lord, I could not handle my trials and tribulation of the world. I came back to see if you were still waiting for my return. I thank you, O'Lord, for being patient with me. This road is so I can't handle it. That's why I turn to you. O'Lord, I know no one but you can heal the sickness of mind. I don't know what to do. Turn left or turn right? I am afraid. No one but you can help me. My past will convict me and I don't want to look back. It's my decision. No one but you, O'Lord. You gave me a chose to love you or to hate you. You never stop loving me and me thank you. No one but you can show that kind of love for someone. O'Lord, you showed your love for me by accepting me back home. No one but you, O' Lord. I thank you and will give You praise. No one but you, O'Lord.

Walter J. Miller

GOD'S WILL

God gave me the wisdom, knowledge, and understanding to write these letters. I will use selective words because I am not a scholar. I have maybe, a fourth grade education. I will try to use words easily read. I will explain, so that my friends can easily understand what I am saying and where I am coming from. With understanding, I want to reach the street people, my peers and those who are less fortunate to get an education in life. Look at the prophets, some were uneducated. With God, even the lowliest without an education, was lifted up to the level of a scholar. As long as you do His will, you will be educated. He will give you courage, wisdom, and knowledge with understanding. You can shine and be a light to the ones who are not educated about God and His will. Maybe they, too, can be a scribe for God, writing down His words to pass them on. I am writing words inspired by Him only; words that would put a joy in your heart just to dictate. Remember Jeremiah and Baruch? Many prophets wrote for God. I am no prophet; however, I was inspired by God, not hired by man to write these letters.

BEING CAREFUL

Since my union with God, I try not to interfere with another person's life unless we are on the same level with God or we have the same spirit. There are descending spirits all around us in this world. Be careful who you spend your time with or who you talk with. God said let not your heart be trouble, for He is with you. So, don't be dismayed by those descending spirits. They are out in the world. People smile at you for many reasons. Some smiles with contempt and some with attempt, trying to temp you for their own reason. Do not be in contempt with them and don't be taken by their smile. The Bible says that you are to entertain strangers for you might be entertaining an Angel. Choices are many but answers are few. It's your choice to ascend or descend in the spirit. My God is an ascending Spirit, which is on high. Your adversary is a descending spirit. So, brothers, ask God for that special gift, to detect those evil spirits. He will. He did it for me. Have faith in Him and pray they won't affect you in any way. They are after your soul. The breath of life that God gave you is His image and goodness. From a friend to a friend.

Walter J. Miller

THE WHOLE SOUL

Have you seen a man without arms or legs? Do you think his God still love him? Do you think he has any place in life? What about people? Do they still look at him as a whole person? Let us look within. What about his spirit? What about his soul? Even though he is only half of a man, a man still has a soul. A whole soul. A man can lose every part of his body, down to his life; however, it's a terrible thing to lose your whole soul. Let us not look at a person for their body, it will perish. Through the grace of God that man has a whole soul. God breathe the breath of life into man, guard it with care for it is the whole soul.

MY GOD IS

My God came to save the ones that were lost. My God came to give me light out of my darkness. My God is my resurrection. I depend on God for everything. He has made me clean. The blind will be able to see with my God's help. My God sent his Son to save me. He is that life giving water. He is my Light and my Good Shepherd. He is my life. I have faith in Jesus. He is my Shepherd. His wisdom is great. He has all powers. He will answer my prayers, if I call on His name and give Him thanks. He gave his life for me and set me free. My God is a forgiving God. He is always working in me. He crossed out all of my debts. He protects me day and night. My God let his Son be that ultimate sacrifice for me.

LIFE FOR THE LIFELESS

Jesus came and died for you, so that the lifeless can have life. He was God's only begotten Son. He gave His life, so that you can have life more abundantly. Would you turn that around if you had all power? Would you, the servant, give your life for your master? He was the Good Shepherd. He died for His sheep. Would you be willing to die for Him? Yes or no? He was the ultimate sacrifice for the whole world. Let us all praise His name for He is the Lord and Savior, Jesus Christ. There was no weapon form against Him that prospered and whatsoever He did prosper. He had the ability of God within himself. He is coming back for all those who kept watch and did not lose faith. He is life for the lifeless. He is the only way that you can have life. So, worship and praise His name unto Zion, His holy mountain. God is good for He is great. I thank Him for being that life for the lifeless.

THE PRICE FOR YESTERDAY

The price I paid for yesterday, I can't add it up today. Maybe things happened in your life to see if you are living by the word of God. There is no price for finding Jesus; He is my yesterday, today and tomorrow. There is no price I can pay God. Yes, He paid a price for me yesterday that I will never be able to pay back. I found God over fifty years ago. Those years were my ever yesterdays. Now, Lord, I must think about tomorrow. You have protected me today and I thank you yesterday. Yes, Lord, if I could pay you for yesterday it would be to serve you yesterday, today, tomorrow and forever, trying to pay off the interest. I can never pay the price for yesterday.

Walter J. Miller

A LETTER TO MY DARLIN'

Dear Darlin',
My Love may this Christmas mean much to you this year in so many ways. God is with you in everything you do. He has blessed you in so many ways you can't count them. Abundantly, He has spread his hand over you. Because you abide in Him, He is abiding in you. Honey, we need to unit together, in the name of Jesus. Darlin', then everything will be alright with us. I think we need to go to Him together and ask for forgiveness for our sins. We need to go before Him. He will keep on blessing us and making you and me strong in His word. Well, Baby, I hope these holidays open your heart to a new world of love for your God. I hope that you continue in spreading His holy name. I love to hear you preach about your God. It really builds me up. I think you are very special to Him.

O'JEHOVAH

O'Jehovah; my God, the Spirit of the most high God, the Father of my Lord and Savior, Jesus Christ, whom I praise and worship. O'Jehovah, how I love thee. You strengthen me. I am down in the valley at the bottom of your holy mountain, looking up to you, O'Jehovah. Please hear my cry; I cry each day for your help and love. Each night my pillow is wet with tears, O'Jehovah. Hear my cry and wipe my tears away. I reach out to you, to strengthen me, in You. By You I can do anything. I thank You for that blessing. It was you who gave your only begotten Son for me. I will praise your name, O'Jehovah.

Repent, Repent, for the time is near.

THE WRONG WAY

Yes! People, it's good to follow Jesus but not the wrong way. To follow in His way is to do as He says. Some are being nail to the cross for their own way, not Jesus. They are symbols of the wrong way. They should be going out and about healing and teaching the way of Jesus. To follow in His footsteps, go and find the lost sheep, fellowship with your brothers and sisters, and strengthen the weak, in Jesus name. Do not get yourself nailed to a wooden cross. That's the wrong way. Yes! Jesus did say pick up your cross and follow me, but not the wrong way. Some has taken following Jesus for their own worldly benefit. You are going to be nailed to the cross by Jesus, in heaven. Jesus said whatever you do in earth, it would be done in heaven. So, let us not take following Jesus the wrong way. The things Jesus went through, no man, I mean no man, can bear, physically or mentally. Let's not punish ourselves trying. Do the things He said to do; keep My commandments, love your neighbor, and feed My sheep. That's the way, not the wrong way.

Walter J. Miller

KEEP ON PRAYING

Keep on praying, even if your petition is not answered. Maybe there is a reason before your God see fit to answer it. Don't lose courage. Some Saints pray for things unseen with no faith. You must believe in your God, in order for Him to hear your prayer. Some lost faith in their God, but some kept on praying. Some pray for better health and they still died. They even pray for more wealth and they end up in poverty. They keep on praying, in the name of Jesus. Keep on praying for there is, a reason and a season for everything to happen. Don't lose faith in your God and in your prayers. Keep on praying. He hears and knows everything you need, even before you ask. Keep on praying in the name of Jesus, for they would be answered. He is a longtime God. If you lose faith in Him, He will not lose faith in you. He loves you. He gave his only Son for you. Keep on praying. Pray to Him for everything, good and bad alike. Forgive all. It could have been a lot worse. Keep on praying. When you pray, don't be like the hypocrites, for they like to pray in churches and stand on street corners so that they can be seen by man. Your God know all and see all. He will award you, if you keep on praying. No matter how hard things get, keep on praying, in the name of Jesus. Keep on praying!

THE CREATOR (Second Time Coming)

The Creator is coming back to create a new earth and a new heaven. Yes! He is coming back to receive all those who stood fast in His word and the ones who kept the faith in the true doctrine. The world was not ready for Him when He came the first time. He is coming back again. How are you going to be really? Saints of God, you that are heirs to the throne, you are princes and princesses and even high priest of the most high God. You are blessed. Don't be caught between the Jews and the Gentiles dilemma. Let your God know that you praise and worship Him in truth and in spirit. Don't be caught up in the world. The creator is coming back for a second time. Not only to receive those who are worthy unto himself, but to judge all those who didn't keep their faith in His word. They did not know that the Lord Jesus was coming back. Yes! The Good Shepherd is coming back to receive His sheep unto himself. Are you ready? Have you repented? Repent, repent, the Creator is coming back. Be not lost my sisters, I pray for you every day, so we may be saved. You have to, however, pray to God for yourself. Being lost when the Lord return will be awful. What a terrible feeling to burn forever. The Creator is coming back.

Walter J. Miller

A GOOD MARRIGAGE IS COMMUNICATION

A husband and wife working in unity with each other is precious and have its joyful moments. What is communication? It is an opinion, a change of ideas and thoughts. Communication builds relationships. It is virtuous, refreshing and praiseworthy. Read Ephesians 4:29-32; Philippians 4:8. Communication is made possible by trust. Understanding qualities like these builds a good relationship and a lifetime marriage. To make it work, it's going to take a genuine commitment and devotion. Two people have chosen each other out of all other human being on this earth. Their desire is to spend the rest of their life together, and to have a helpmate; some one that is of good humor, affection, discreet, forgiving, joyful and with the patience of the Almighty. Godly qualities will adorn your marriage. Having good communication is very important. It would help you avoid, bitterness, dislike and anger. Good communication will help with the endurance of; until death do us part. It will help you overcome all obstacles. I believe that a true companion is God sent. Read Proverbs 17:17; Ephesians 4:26; Proverbs 30:33; Ecclesiastes 3:1-7; Colossians 4:6; Proverbs 16:23; and Genesis 2:18-21.

BEING A FISHERMAN

O'Lord, here I am sitting on the bank of the river. I'm looking at your wonderful creation; the river, the sea, the sky, and the sun. How the sun guides the world by day and the moon take over at night, along with the stars. O'Lord, here I am trying to catch a fish, to feed myself. I want to be a fisherman like Jesus was, a fisher of man. He was a real fisherman. There were not one fish smarter than He. Now, that's being a fisherman. O'Lord, if I can catch just one fish, I know that you would be happy for me. If, I can catch one fish of man then I know I would be a fisherman. Teach me, O'Lord, to fish for the lost souls that are caught up in the net of the world. Little ones and big ones alike, I want to save them all. Being a fisherman you have to know about the tides, where the fish are biting and how to catch them. That's being a fisherman.

For I have the ability of Jesus within me. For I am an overcomer of the world. For whatsoever I do will proper, in the name of Jesus.

Walter J. Miller

TELLING IT LIKE IT IS

O'Lord, in my every day struggle, I am catching hell. I am trying to do the right thing and follow in your footsteps, for I am weak. There are things in my life that need to be move out of my life. This demonic spirit, O'Lord, remove this evil away from me. It keeps me away from you. O'Lord, I am asking you to take this spirit and cast it into the sea. It burns deep down in my soul. O'Lord, only you can help me. Please Father, do it for me and I will praise your name unto the holy mountain. I have no friends, only you. I am sorry of my sins. Please forgive me. I want to tell the world of your love for me. You died for me so that I may live. I thank you for removing these stumbling blocks out of my way. Only you, O'Lord can do all this for you are the Almighty. I am telling it like it is. Your love is never ending. I thank you for that precious love. I am telling it like it is.

LISTEN TO THE SPIRIT

There are times when my God would try to get my attention by telling me what is right or wrong. I refused to listen until I am in real trouble. I know it would be the Spirit of Jesus. He brought me out of the things that would happen to me. I can't explain it. I know it was the Spirit of God trying to tell me the right way to go. He was showing me things in the Spirit. My God and I are real close friends. We are the best of friends. We walk and talk to each other every day. I thank Him for being there for me; guiding my footsteps and helping me bridle my tongue. Sometimes, I have a hard time with the Spirit controlling my tongue. I pray every day for that change. This demonic spirit within me is keeping away from his Spirit and cutting out my blessing. I ask my God to remove this evil spirit away from me. I will listen to what the Spirit is saying. With my fasting and praying, He will help me listen to the Spirit.

PARALYZED

The roads to Hell are smooth and the road to God is real rough. Just think of a man being put on a stretcher, paralyzed. He would have to depend on others for his safety. I was that man, paralyzed by sin. I was carried over rough roads in my life. Then, I had a spiritual awakening. I asked God, to ask life to let me go, so that I could be healed. I had traveled the path of Hell. The Holy Spirit convicted me of that life. I was a sinner. I rested from God and He did the same from me. He was always ready, however, to help me by giving me His hand. When I am tired, I learn to work for Him and He will work for me. That was my blessing from Him, not keeping me paralyzed in my sin. I thank Him every day.

Walter J. Miller

PROMISE KEEPING

Lord, you said that if I obey you. You would take care and protect me. When I pass through deep waters, I will not be swallowed up. I will be like Shadrach, Meshach and Abednego; I will not get burnt by the fire. Those are your promises. My promise is to follow you wherever you lead me. You will be my Protector and my Defender. Lord, you showed me your love in so many ways. How can I hold you to all of this? O'Lord, I thank you for it. I thank you for not making me too stubborn to obey you. I am glad that you opened my eyes to see your glory. You opened my ears so that I can hear your friendly voice when you call my name. Lord, you put in my heart, all the love I have for my brothers and sisters. Please teach me to be more understanding, by giving me wisdom and knowledge. Help me to keep your commandments and never let go of your face and image. Lord, keep me walking in your likeness so that I can be content and patient. Help me to be still when you talk so that I can hear every word you say.

WHAT A FRIEND

I can recall the times that I did not have food to eat, clothes to put on my back, or shoes to wear. I went to my sister, my mother, and some of my so call friends. They did me no good. Out of all my trust in them, they refuse to help me. I went to a Friend I had left behind, a friend I had betrayed for my other so call friends. I cried as I went, not knowing whether my Friend would be there for me, in my hard times. I was wrong, my friends and family betrayed me. I was so ashamed to go back to the Best Friend I had left behind. I still see some of those same friends, still doing the same things today, betraying others. Finally I went back to the true Friend and with open arms, He welcome me back. He forgave me for all my wrongs. I never believe a True Friend would smile on me and say welcome home. He gave me food to eat, new clothes to wear, and new shoes, so that I can have a new walk. He, also, put a new song upon my lips. When I pass by those same friends, my sister and my mother, they look with awe. How can someone be such a friend to do all this? What a Friend! Trust in the Lord for He is your Best Friend. Don't depend on the people of this world. They are only friends to themselves. I thank God for being my friend. What a Friend!

Walter J. Miller

TRADITIONALLY SPEAKING

It would be very hypocritical to say that I am getting in the spirit of Christmas. I stay in the spirit. Getting in the spirit is what the heathens and religious people do. They get in the spirit once a year for the birth of their God. Once a week they praise Him on Sunday like the hypocrites do. If they only study and show themselves approved, they would learn that God made all days; Monday, Tuesday, Wednesday, Thursday, Friday, Saturday and Sunday, as well.

God made them all and was pleased with them all. He rested on Sunday. Men follow in the traditions of other men before them, not knowing the truth of his tradition. The blind is leading the blind. They should be following the way of Jesus. Traditionally speaking, they are following a myth. They are keeping the traditional alive for their own propose and selfish desires. They keep swaying and betraying God's people. Why do they keep on living this tradition? Traditionally speaking, my God, Lord and Savior, Jesus Christ was born over 2500 years ago. He died for my sins and was raise back to life by God Almighty. To this day He is yet alive. You cannot recreate something that was always and will always be. Be not followers of these people for they will lead you to serve other gods instead of the God Almighty. I am traditionally speaking. I praise and worship my God every day, not just on Sunday or on Christmas.
Man has led so many of God's Saints away with their traditionally speaking ways.

FATHER GOD #2

Father God, in the name of Jesus, I thank you for answering my prayer. Father God, I want you to bless me. I know that I am in this battle. I am not alone for I know that you are with me. I have on your whole armor which is my protection. This warfare is between me and my enemy which is the devil, the adversary of the whole world. He is against everything that the Almighty God stands for. Satan can give you almost everything that the Almighty God can, however, Lucifer can't give you eternal life. This is my prayer unto you, O'God. Reach out your ever loving hand and cover me. Lord, cover me in the noon day. I love your ways for they are a turban and a necklace unto my body. I will carry them around my waist as a sash and in my heart as a light. Father God, I praise your name for it is sweet upon my lips. Father God, I want you to guide me. I love this personal relation that we have. Now that we can talk face to face, you are my best friend. You are my shelter doing the storm and I thank you. Father God, I thank you for the many blessings that you have bestowed upon me. You changed my life from my addiction and you never left me alone. You sent one of your angels into my life. Father God, teach me how to love, in the name of Jesus. Father God!

IDENTIFICATION RECORD Local Number: 12 453		ST. LUCIE COUNTY SHERIFF'S OFFICE FORT PIERCE, FLORIDA
Name: Walter James Miller	DOB: 6-6-48	Alias:
Name Used & Number:	Date:	Charge: Key to Charges: (F)=Felony,(M)=Misdemeanor,(D)=Domestic
Walter James Miller	9-24-90	Theft (M) 90-2130M
Walter James Miller	5-31-91	Violation of provisional release (Purchase of marijuana) for Division of Corrections
Walter James Miller	11-9-91 FPPD	1) Prowling 2) Possession of drug paraphernalia
Walter James Miller	12-27-92 FPPD	Prowling
Walter James Miller	4-10-93 FPPD	1) Possession of controlled substance (cocaine) 93-820CF 2) Possession of marijuana (M) 3) Possession of drug paraphernalia
Walter James Miller	9-9-93	Possession of drug paraphernalia 93-2009MM
Walter James Miller	12-11-94	1) Possession of controlled substance (cocaine) 93-820CF 2) Possession of drug paraphernalia
Walter James Miller	1-11-95 FPPD	1) Delivery of cocaine 95-92CF 2) Possession of controlled substance (cocaine) 3) Delivery of cocaine 95-92CF 4) Possession of controlled substance (cocaine)
Walter James Miller	3-22-97 FPPD	Possession of controlled substance with intent to sell (cocaine)

IDENTIFICATION RECORD Local Number: 12 453		ST. LUCIE COUNTY SHERIFF'S OFFICE FORT PIERCE, FLORIDA	
Name: Walter James Miller	DOB: 6-6-48	Alias:	
Name Used & Number:	Date:	Charge: Key to Charges: (F)=Felony, (M)=Misdemeanor, (D)=Domestic	

Name Used & Number	Date	Charge
Walter James Miller	4-5-88 FPPD	1) Obstructing Justice 2) Possession of controlled substance (cocaine)
Walter James Miller	5-14-88 FPPD	2) Possession of controlled substance (cocaine)
Walter James Miller	5-19-88 FPPD	1) Delivery of cocaine 2) Possession of controlled substance (cocaine)
Walter James Miller	6-29-88 FPPD	1) Possession of drug paraphernalia 2) Possession of controlled substance (cocaine)
Walter James Miller	7-24-88 FPPD	1) Possession of marijuana (M) 88-2154MM 2) Resisting arrest without violence
Walter James Miller	8-16-88 FPPD	1) Delivery of marijuana 2) Delivery of marijuana
Walter James Miller	8-21-88	1) Violation of Probation (Delivery of cocaine) 87-3266CF 2) Violation of Probation (Possession of cocaine) 87-2681CF
Walter James Miller	7-8-89 FPPD	Delivery of cocaine
Walter James Miller	8-8 Violation	1) Violaton of Probation (Delivery of marijuana) 2) Violation of Probation (Delivery of marijuana)
Walter James Miller	8-31-90 FPPD	Burglary

IDENTIFICATION RECORD Local Number: 12 453	ST. LUCIE COUNTY SHERIFF'S OFFICE FORT PIERCE, FLORIDA	
Name: Walter James Miller	DOB: 6-6-48	Alias:
Name Used & Number:	Date:	Charge: Key to Charges: (F)=Felony, (M)=Misdemeanor, (D)=Domestic
Walter James Miller	10-15-97 FPPD	1) Theft (M) 97-3647MM 2) Possession of drug paraphernalia 3) Possession of controlled substance (cocaine) 97-3017CF
Walter James Miller	6-27-98 FPPD	1) Possession of controlled substance (cocaine) 2) Possession of drug paraphernalia 3) Resisting officer without violence 4) Violation of Probation 97-3647MM (Possession of drug paraphernalia)

IDENTIFICATION RECORD Local Number: 12 453		ST. LUCIE COUNTY SHERIFF'S OFFICE FORT PIERCE, FLORIDA	
Name: Walter James Miller	*DOB:* 6-6-48	*Alias:*	
Name Used & Number:	Date:	Charge: Key to Charges: (F)=Felony, (M)=Misdemeanor, (D)=Domestic	

Name	Date	Charge
Walter James Miller	2-21-71	Disorderly conduct (riot)
Walter James Miller	1-3-74	Assault & Battery
Walter James Miller	10-25-74	Applicant Print, Deputy Sheriff
Walter James Miller	8-27-79 FPPD	1) Dealing in stolen property 2) Disorderly conduct
Walter James Miller	8-28-79	Disorderly conduct (2 counts)
Walter James Miller	8-29-80	No driver license
Walter James Miller	6-21-86 FPPD	1) Theft (M) 2) Theft (M)
Walter James Miller	10-1-86 FPPD	Battery 86-2613M
Walter James Miller	3-16-87 FPPD	1) Violation of Probation (Battery) 86-2613M 2) Violation of Probation (Theft) 86-2030M 3) Violation of Probation (Theft) 86-2029M
Walter James Miller	9-16-87 FPPD	1) Soliciting for prostitution 87-2681 CF-A 2) Possession of controlled substance (cocaine)
Walter James Miller	11-24-87 FPPD	1) Delivery of cocaine 87-3266CF 2) Possession of controlled substance (cocaine)

Walter J. Miller

From a sinner to a winner, through the grace of my God. I am on the winning team. My Lord brought me from death to life again. I once was dead unto my God. He inspired me to write these spiritual letters and poems through His grace and mercy. The love of God keeps me. I know without that Love, I would be nothing. He guides me daily in all things. From a sinner to a winner; I am thankful. If it had not been for the blood of Jesus, it would be impossible. My brothers and sisters; stop being a sinner and be a winner, in Jesus name. Many times I knew that my life was over, but not Jesus. He saw to it that I lived. My Lord and Savior covered me with His blood. I will let no weapon form against me prosper. Thank you, Jesus. I praise and worship you for you are my Defender. I ask you to strengthen me against the wiles of this world daily. I want my brothers and sisters to receive the crown that my God has for them. There were times when I wanted to leave my brothers and sisters behind; however, I asked my God to give me strength. With wisdom, knowledge and understanding, I can go back and get my brothers and sisters.

From a Sinner to a Winner

www.ingramcontent.com/pod-product-compliance
Lightning Source LLC
Chambersburg PA
CBHW051648040426
42446CB00009B/1036